Cover image:
Mirror
ca. 1550–1458 B.C.
New Kingdom, Egypt
© The Metropolitan Museum

This issue is supported in part by:

NORTHWESTERN
UNIVERSITY
IN QATAR

ARABLIT QUARTERLY

VOLUME 5, ISSUE 1
Spring 2022

Editor-in-chief: M Lynx Qualey
Art Director: Hassân Al Mohtasib
Contributing Editors:
Nashwa Gowanlock, Sawad Hussain,
Olivia Snaije, Nariman Youssef,
Lucie Taylor, Joel Mitchell,
Ranya Abdel Rahman
Editorial Assistant:
Leonie Rau
Research Consultant:
Amanda Hannoosh Steinberg

A production of www.arablit.org
Opinions, submissions, advertising:
info@arablit.org
© All rights reserved

ر / أ / ي

Ra' – Hamza – Ya'

© Larisa Birta, Unsplash

◆ **INTRODUCTION**
4   by M Lynx Qualey

◆ **FEATURES**

8   **Squaring & Circling the Mirror**
By Al-Jahiz
translated by Michael Payne

18   **Talking Mirrors: Bodies and Dis-ease**
By Shahd Alshammari

26   **My Face Through the Seasons**
By Mohamed Choukri
translated by Jonas Elbousty

82   **'Mother of Happy Endings'**
By Nawal Nasrallah

◆ **SHORT FICTION**

40   **Sad Woman's Mirror**
By Maheera Migdadi
translated by Madeline Edwards

44   **Glass**
By Rema Hmoud
translated by Ibrahim Fawzy

46   **Closer Than They Appear**
By Enas Eltorky

◆ **STORY PRIZE**

66   **How Kind They Are**
By Mustafa Taj Aldeen Almosa
translated by Maisaa Tanjour & Alice Holttum

70   **You Can Call Me Velvet**
by Rasha Abbas
translated by Katharine Halls

74   **The Baffling Case of the Man Called Ahmet Yilmaz**
By Karima Ahdad
translated by Katherine Van de Vate

78   **The Hemingway Man**
By Ahmed Magdy Hammam
translated by Burnaby Hawkes

82   **Camphor Forestland**
By Said Takieddine
translated by Dima El-Mouallem

◆ **POETRY**

6   **Hearsay at the Yahya Market**
By Ra'ad Abdulqadir
Translated by Shakir Mustafa

16   **Loneliness**
By Ali Ja'far Al-Allaq
translated by Shakir Mustafa

24   **From 'On to the Next Room'**
By Abdalrahman Alqalaq
translated by Sara Abou Rashed

38   **Reflection**
By Rym Jalil
translated by Nawara Belal

50   **Heads / Tails**
By Reem Abbas

52   **The Only Stranger Here**
By Duna Ghali
translated by Layla AlAmmar

56   **Ash-sha'b Yurid Isqat an-Nizam**
By Hilal Badr
translated by Ghada Alatrash

60   **The Patient Mirror**
By Qassim Majeed
translated by Zeena Faulk

PAGE 50

Heads / Tails

Introduction

In the story "Of Prince Zayn al-Asnam and the King of the Djinn," published in the eighth volume of Antoine Galland's *Les mille et une nuit, contes arabes,* an orphaned prince receives a gift from the king of the djinn: a magic mirror. Young Zayn must use this mirror to find a virgin (human) girl, who he is to turn over to the djinn ruler. In exchange for this celibate teen, the djinn promises to cough up the location of the great treasure that belonged to Zayn's late father.

The magic of this particular mirror is that the prince can hold it up to any young woman and discover, with a quick glance at her reflection, whether she has had any unlawful relationships with men. Zayn uses it to view all the unmarried women of Cairo and is, naturally, disappointed in his quest. Thus he must travel to Baghdad to find one untouched adolescent. (When he does find her, Zayn does not turn her over to the djinn, but rather marries the precious, un-precocious commodity.)

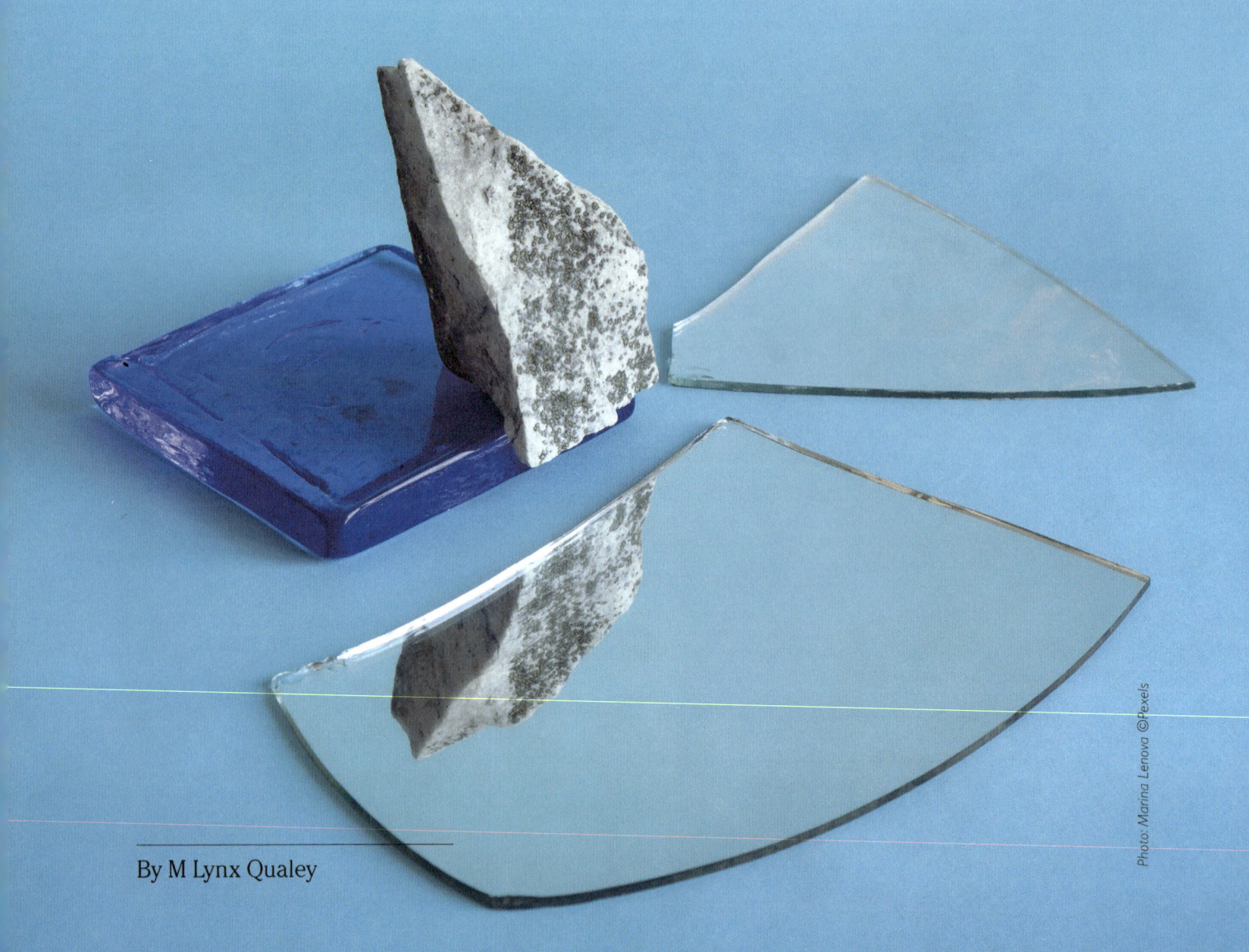

By M Lynx Qualey

Perhaps Antoine Galland's publisher was hoping that the old man wouldn't page all the way to the end of this volume. But apparently he did. Thus, in the ninth volume of *Les mille et une nuit,* the French scholar-translator opens with an announcement that the final two stories in Vol. 8—the Zayn al-Asnam tale and one other—were slipped in without his knowledge. These two tales were translated from a Turkish collection, *Ferec ba'de Şidde,* by Galland's colleague, François Petis de la Croix.

The Turkish collection was probably translated from one titled *al-Faraj ba'd al-shidda,* although the Turkish tales are unlike al-Tanukhi's famous "relief after adversity" stories. The *Ferec* stories, according to scholar Hakan Karateke, were probably translated from a Persian collection that is now lost. Also, Karateke adds in "The Politics of Translation: Two Stories from the Turkish *Ferec ba'de Şidde* in *Les mille et une nuit, contes arabes,"* there was no mirror in the Turkish tale. The translator invented it.

"Zayn al-Asnam" is thus an Orientalist reflection, a falsified relic that's part Shahrazade, part Snow White. And yet the prince's mirror-tale has persisted in its relationship to the *Nights*, appearing in an echoing English, in the second volume of *The Arabian Nights' Entertainments*, as well as in Richard Burton's *Supplemental Nights*.

In de la Croix's version of the story, the djinn's mirror purports to tell a truth that humans cannot see with eyes alone. In this issue, our thirteenth, there is a mirror with similar properties in Enas Eltorky's surreal, Sufi-esque "Closer Than They Appear." But in Eltorky's short story, when the mystic's mirror reflects the naked truth, we don't get a royal wedding or happily-ever-after. Instead, the community's social fabric swiftly unravels.

Throughout this issue, the mirror is an uneasy metaphor for truth, just as it is an uneasy metaphor for translation. Kuwaiti scholar and memoirist Shahd Alshammari reflects on what the mirror can—and can't—tell us about the disabled self. In her essay, "Talking Mirrors: Bodies and Dis-ease," she recalls Sylvia Plath's description of the mirror as "silver and exact." Yet she experiences the mirror's supposed honesty less as exactness and more as an insistence to conformity: that she must look and walk and smile the same as some imagined ideal.

A mirror is not always unwelcome. In ninth-century Basra, al-Jahiz was interested in the scientific and philosophical properties of mirrors, and he wrote about them in *Kitab al-Tarbi' wa-l-tadwir,* an excerpt of which is translated by Michael Payne for this issue. In thirteenth-century Andalusia, Nawal Nasrallah tells us in her essay "Mother of Happy Endings," a mirror was used in making sweet-savory chicken pie. But if medievals used their rare and precious mirrors for philosophy, cookery, divination, and trickery (as in al-Jawbari's thirteenth-century *Book of Charlatans*), the contemporary writers in this issue seem surrounded, haunted, and beset by reflective surfaces.

In Rema Hmoud's "Glass," here translated by Ibrahim Fawzy, the narrator is haunted by her image distorted in reflections, while other women's faces appear normal. In Maheera Migdadi's "Sad Woman's Mirrors," reflective surfaces follow the protagonist everywhere, until she stares into a puddle and asks plaintively: "In this entire universe, isn't there one mirror, one shiny reflective thing, that makes me look pretty?"

In the pieces included here, men seem more likely to link mirrors to a past, while for women they are part of an encircling present. Yet it is not only women who shy from mirrors. The great Moroccan writer Mohamed Choukri's reflections in "My Face Through the Seasons," translated by Jonas Elbousty, opens with: "*We didn't have a mirror at home, / because none of us wanted to see his face in it.*" And in Abdalrahman Alqalaq's poem "On to the Next Room," here translated by Sara Abou Rashed, one of the characters who is constantly on the move opens a suitcase "and takes out a mirror and a watch. / Neither of you can bear the presence / of these two objects at once."

In this issue, we also have the four stories that were shortlisted for the 2021 ArabLit Story Prize as well as the winner, Mustafa Taj Aldeen Almosa's "How Kind They Are," translated by Maisaa Tanjour and Alice Holttum. The translations were judged not only for their vibrancy, wit, emotional depth, and originality, but also for how they mirrored their originals. Yet this mirroring does not mean a one-to-one correspondence.

In a video interview with AUC Press, the late Humphrey Davies said, in response to a question about whether he "mirrored" an author's style, "I like the idea of mirrors and reflecting. But you see, a mirror [image] is not identical. It's subtly changed." (Or, as in the case of François Petis de la Croix, the change is not subtle at all.)

Translations also can be multiple, and broken mirrors can reflect a more salutary—and interesting—multiplicity of meanings. In Alshammari's "Talking Mirrors," it is the broken mirrors that make her feel safe, as they "help us see wholeness in lack." And in Reem Abbas's encantatory poem "Heads/Tails," tongues are refracted, and there are: "Chinks & shards: healing the colonial / wound is a museum of mirrors."

Mirrors, once precious, have become ubiquitous. We hope this collection of works brings back a little of their medieval magic.

Poetry

Hearsay at the Yahya Market

By **Ra'ad Abdulqadir**

Translated by
Shakir Mustafa

The Yahya market was buzzing. The god, some said, would brandish his weapons in the closing third of the night.

Candle sellers prepared for the event, and mirror sellers set their mirrors on the roads. The perfumers opened their empty canisters to catch the stray smell.

Given the treachery of speculation, the real treachery would be in the pointless wait. The mirrors might not show him, and the canisters might not contain him.

But where does all this awesome beauty come from? And all this strange, overwhelming scent?

في سوق يحيى كانت الشائعات يقال ان الإله سينزل في ذلك الليل الأخير. ليلوح بأسلحته

باعة الشموع استعدوا للحدث باعة المرايا نصبوا مراياهم في الطرقات العطارون فتحوا زجاجاتهم القارغة ليقتنصوا عطره الشارد.

قد يكون من الصعب التوقع ستكون الخيبة أصعب قد لا يظهر في مراياهم، قد لا تقتنصه زجاجاتهم.

ولكن من أين كل هذا الجمال المبهج وما هذه الرائحة الزكية الغريبة؟

Baghdad. Copper bazaar. 1932 © Library of Congress

المعهد الفرنسي بدمشق
للدراسات العربية

كتاب
التربيع والتدوير
للجاحظ

عُنيَ بنشرِه وتحقيقِه
شارل پلّات
أستاذ بمدرسة اللغات الشرقية الحيّة
بباريس

دمشق
١٩٥٥

Excerpt

Squaring & Circling the Mirror

By **Al-Jahiz**

Translated by
Michael Payne

التربيع والتدوير

In what has been described as his "most baffling composition," al-Jahiz (d. 868–869) wrote an extended passage on mirrors. The book in which it is included, *Kitab al-Tarbi' wa-l-tadwir* (*The Book of Squaring and Circling*), is an exhausting series of questions intended to ridicule and insult its opponent and addressee, a Shi'i bureaucrat named Ahmad b. 'Abd al-Wahhab. The premise of the book is that Ahmad had described himself as tall, but al-Jahiz thought otherwise and proceeded to denigrate Ahmad's body before posing a succession of difficult questions to belittle and confound him. Al-Jahiz was a Mu'tazili philosopher and litterateur who has been called "the greatest humanist in the Arab tradition" and "the father of Arabic prose," but we can call him something else as well: a troll.

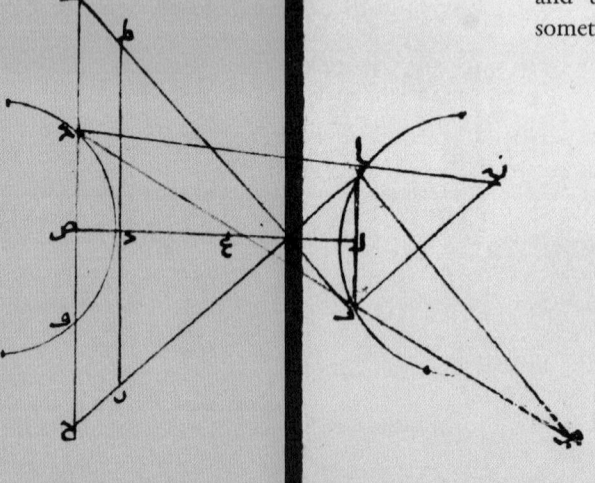

The Book of Squaring and Circling is an inquisition, a taunt, and an admonition. On its face, the text is fundamentally an artifact of mockery—it is a book-length insult—but the substance of the questions tells us something about his contemporaries' debates in the sciences and philosophy. Al-Jahiz pesters his reader with complex questions about the nature of rainbows, the origin of giraffes, and the appearance of comets. His section on mirrors is a densely layered interrogation about vision, optics, colors, and reflective surfaces. Throughout the work, few answers are provided, because the book is neither an imagined debate nor an invitation to dialogue. It is, instead, an assertion of dominion.

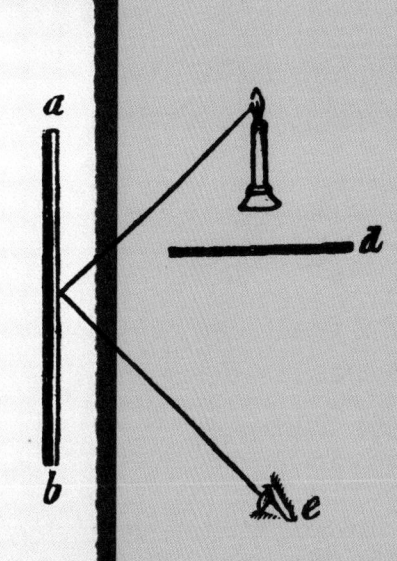

———

للجاحظ

167 Tell me about mirrors. How is it that they show faces while creation is viewed in them, as with anything smooth and polished or clear and calm: a sword, a metal mirror, bottles, still water, even glistening ink—a black pupil if the observer in the pupil is white, or a milky pupil if the observer in it is black? How is it that running water; a burning fire; or the sun, endowed with rays, do not admit a form nor fix creation within them?

168 And about the theory held by those who claim that waning is not a permanent state of the moon, that something inert does not change color, and that blackness does not remain. Rather, it is a thing into which people peer—because it is polished smooth—by facing the earth and what is in it. Just as when someone who is facing the pupil sees a human form, and there's no actual form. Yet this is something that exists when facing a thing. And why is it that some mirrors show the face and the nape and some show the head inverted? And why don't you ever find writing on screens or covers that isn't flipped?

كتاب التربيع والتدوير ٨٩

ولا كَمَد جامد ولا سَواد واكد ، وإنّما ذلك شيءٌ رآه الناس فيه إذ(١) كان أملسَ صقيلًا ، بمقابلة الأرض وما فيها ، كما يرى مَن قابلَ الحدقة صورةَ إنسان وليس هناك صورة ، وإنّما هو شيء. يوجد عند المقابلة ؟ ولمَ صار بعضُ المرائي يُري الوجهَ والقَفا ويرى الرأسَ منكّساً ؟ ولمَ كنتَ لا تجد كتاب الستور والمطارح فيها أبدًا إلّا مقلوباً ؟

١٦٩ ـ وما تلك الصورة الثابتة في المرآة : أَعَرَضٌ أم جوهرٌ أم شيء(٢) وحقيقة أم تخييل ؟ والذي ترى ، أهو وجهك أو غير وجهك ؟ فإن كان عَرَضاً ، فما الذي ولّده وما الذي أوجبَه ، والوجه لم يُماسَّه ولم يعمل فيه ؟ وهل أبطلت تلك الصورةُ المرئيةُ صورةَ مكانِها في المرآة ، ولمَ ، وأنت لستَ تراه في نفس صفيحة المرآة ، ولمَ ، وكأنّك تراها في هواءٍ خلفَ جوفِها ؟

١٧٠ ـ وهل أبطل ذلك اللون الذي هو في مثال لونك لونَ المرآة ؟ فإن لم يكن أبطله فهناك إذاً صورتان في جسمٍ واحدٍ(٣) أو لونان في جوهرٍ واحدٍ ؟ وإن كان قد أبطل لون الحديد ، فكيف أبطله من غير أن يكون عَمِلَ فيه ؟ وكيف يعمل فيه وحيّزُه غير حيّزه وهو لا مُماسٌّ ولا متصل ولا مصادم ؟ وسواءٌ ذكرنا صفيحة الحديد أم ما خلّفَها من الهواء وما قدّامَها من الفُرجة ، كلَّ ذلك جسمٌ ذو لون ؟ فإن اعتللتَ بالشعاع الفاصل ، والشعاع

---

١) س : اذ ؛ ف و م : إذا .
٢) ف و م : شي. ؛ س : أي شي. .
٣) س : في حال واحد ؛ ف و م : في حال .

كتاب التربيع والتدوير

١٦٦ ـ وستقول(١) : « ما دعـاك إلى التنويه بذِكري وتعريف الناس مكاني ، وقد تعرف حِشْمَتي وانقباضي ونفوري(٢) واستيحاشي ؟ » ؛ ولولا أنك ـ جعلت فِـداك ـ مسؤول في كلّ زمان والغـاية في كلّ دهر ، لَمَا أفردتُك(٣) بهـذا الكتاب ولَمَا أطمعتُ نفسي في الجواب ؛ ولكنك قد كنتَ أذنت في مثلها لِهرْمِس ثم لإفلاطون ثم لأرسطاطاليس ، ثمّ أَجَبْتَ مَعْبَـد الجُنّي وغَيْلان الـدِمَشقيّ وعمرو بن عُبَيْد وواصِل بن عَطاء وابراهيم بن سَيّار وعليّ بن خالد الأُسواري ؛ فتربيَة كفّك والناشئ تحت جَناحك أحقُّ بذلك وأولى ، وقد كان يجب أن تكون على ذلك أحرَصَ به وأعنى .

٭٭٭

١٦٧ ـ وخبِّرْني عن المَراني وكيف صارت ترى الوجوه وتُبصَر فيها الخَلْق ، وكذلك كلّ أمْلَسَ صَقيل وصافٍ ساكن كالسيف والوَذيلة والقوارير والماء الراكد ، حتى الجَبَر البرّاق والحَدقة السوداء ـ إذا كان الناظر في الحدقة أبيضَ ـ ، والحدقة المُغْرَبة ـ إذا كان الناظر فيهـا أسوَدَ ـ ؟ و كيف صار الماء الجاري والنار الملتهبة(٤) والشمس ذات الشُّعاع لا تقبل الصورة ولا يثبت فيها الخَلق ؟

١٦٨ ـ وعن قول مَن زعم أنـه ليس في القمر مَحْقٌ ثابت

---

١) ف و م : وستقول ؛ س : وستقول .
٢) س : نفوري ؛ ف و م : نفردي .
٣) ف و م و س : نفردتك .
٤) م و س : الملتهبة ؛ ف : المتلهبة .

كتاب التربيع والتدوير   ٩١

اشتدّ صوتُه بلا باب، والصوت لا بدّ له من هواء   وإذا اشتدّ فلا بدّ له من باب؟ وما تقول(١) في خضر السماء: أهو خضر جلَدها كما نقول(٢)   أم ذلك لحرّ الهواء كما يقول خصمُنا؟

١٧٤ _ وهل ترُعم أن الأفلاك ذات لون؟ فإن كان لها لون، فقد احتملت جميع الأشكال   وهذا خلافُ ما يقولون؛ وإن لم تكن ذات لون فالسماء إذًا غير الفلك، فهـذا هذا؛ ونقول أيضاً: إن كنّا لا نرى القرى المستطيلة البنيان(٣) المختلفة [الشكل] من البعد إلّا مستديرة، فلعلّ الشمس مُصلَّبـة   والكواكب مربَّعة!

١٧٥ _ وما تقول في المدّ والجزر: أمِن مَلَك يضع رجلًا ويرفع رجلًا؟ فإن كان كذلك فلعلّ مديّر الفلك مَلَك، ولعلّ صوت الرعد صوتُ زَجر مَلَك! فتَدَع الفلسفة   ونأخذ بقول الجماعة، أم تزعم أن المدّ والجزر من نفس الجواذب إذا جذب [القمر] وإذا دفع(٤)؟ وما تقول في قول مَن زعم أن القمر مائي   وأشبه الكواكب بطبيعة النار، فإنما يكون الجزر والمدّ على مقادير جذبه للماء   وإرساله له؟ ذلك معروف في منازله ومجاريه، يعرف ذلك أهل الجزر والمد.

١٧٦ _ خبّرني كيف صارت القيافة في النّسبة   وفي الماء

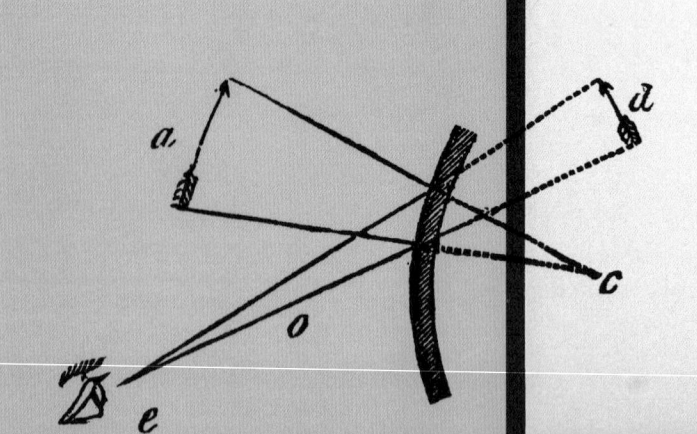

---

(١) ف و م: تقول؛   : نقول.
(٢) ف و م: نقول؛ س: تقول.
(٣) ف و م: والبنيان؛ س: البنيان.
(٤) ف و م و س: رفع.

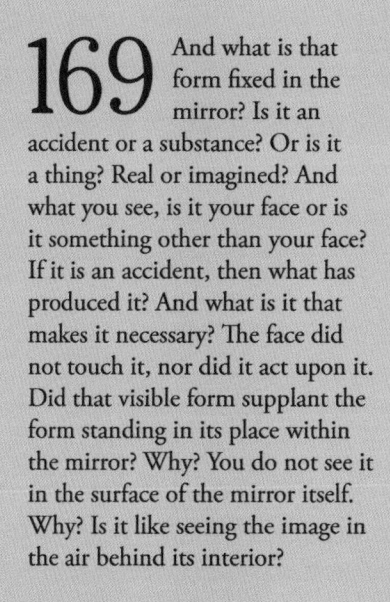

169 And what is that form fixed in the mirror? Is it an accident or a substance? Or is it a thing? Real or imagined? And what you see, is it your face or is it something other than your face? If it is an accident, then what has produced it? And what is it that makes it necessary? The face did not touch it, nor did it act upon it. Did that visible form supplant the form standing in its place within the mirror? Why? You do not see it in the surface of the mirror itself. Why? Is it like seeing the image in the air behind its interior?

170 Did that color, which is so like yours, supplant the color of the mirror? If it does not supplant it, then there are two forms in a single body, and two colors in a single substance. And if it did supplant the color of the iron, then how did it supplant it without acting upon it? And how did it act upon it? The space that it occupies is not the space occupied by another. It is neither touching, nor continuous, nor interacting. Whether we mention the iron surface, the air behind it, or the aperture before it, all of these are bodies possessing color. If you suggest that the cause is the rays emitted by the eye, and the rays differ in sensation—like the organ that perceives and that which is perceived—how do we see what is different? How, when rays are color and whiteness, does the sensitive soul not perceive them with something of their senses?

Poetry

Loneliness

By **Ali Ja'far Al-Allaq**

Translated by
Shakir Mustafa

Flowers, I brought for my friends
and compassion to the stones.
Crying, I came to a brook,
drying in loneliness. Songs
are in ruins, and lovers
mere mirrors, almost broken.

No horses
cross waterways at sunsets,
and mirrors look like shallow brooks.

جئتُ أدعو لأصدقائي بالورد
وأحنو على الصخى جئتُ أبكي
لغدير يجفّ
دون معزوفة الأغاني
خرائب، والعشّاق مرايا
كسيرة.

لا خيول
تعبر الماء في الغسَقِ العربانِ
كنّقايا الغدرانِ..

Levi Meir Clancy © Unsplash

Essay

Bodies and Disease

Talking Mirros

By **Shahd Alshammari**
Artwork by **A.Sh.**

To have a body at all is to be carrying shame.
To have a woman's body is to carry a gendered shame. To have a disabled woman's body
is to carry an even more specific, complex shame,
constantly being made aware of lack. Lack in a very real and material sense, away from
all abstract thought and theories of the body.

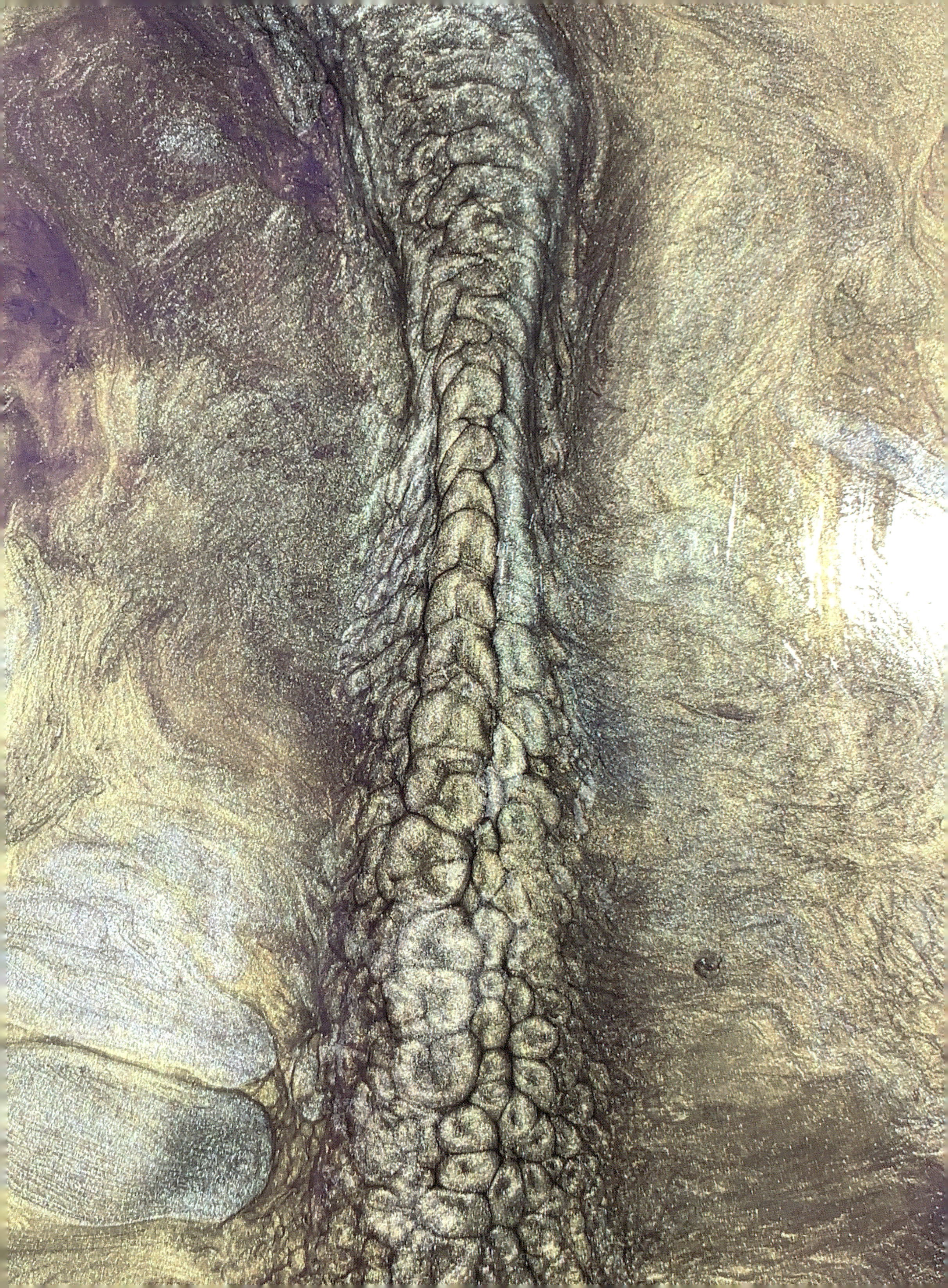

Like most girls, I grew up unaware of my body until puberty hit and the changes were obvious. But these changes were celebrated, not a cause for concern. They were not changes that I would avoid looking at. Mirrors became my friend, a place I could look for reaffirmation of my status as a woman, of being beautiful, and finally, like many girls, I started carrying one—one never knew when it might come in handy.

In her poem "Mirror," Sylvia Plath simplifies the mirror's identity: "I am silver and exact. I have no preconceptions." I believe her. I've always believed Plath. Mirrors have no preconceptions. They don't carry cultural ideologies of femininity. But people do. With time, and as I began to see that there was no avoiding the physical changes that came with having a disabled body, I began to reconsider my relationship with mirrors. I have thought continually, obsessively, and incessantly about that object, *silver and exact*. My latest book, *Head Above Water*, deals with society's stigmatization of disability and illness, and, in it, I hold a mirror up to society's shaming of ill bodies. Because it is nonfiction, I draw on my experiences navigating the world as a woman living with a disability. I retaliate against the multiple (and very vocal) mirrors that refused to let me believe I could belong safely inside my disabled body. From the book:

> Mirrors are tools that measure the death of our skin, and the dark circles under my eyes became another way to remind me that I was aging faster than my friends. My eyes constantly looked tired no matter how many hours I slept. I was continuously embarrassed by the number of comments I received about my lack of makeup, my sleepy red eyes, and I began anticipating the comments before anyone ever said anything. The amount of makeup I tried to use to cover my fatigued eyes didn't do me any good. Instead, I looked ghost-like and as washed out as a tie-dyed shirt that had gone bad.

I wasn't the only disabled person preoccupied with mirrors. When I read Aziz Mohammed's *The Critical Case of a Man Called K*, I felt less alone. The narrator, struggling with leukemia, cannot help but check his reflection in the mirror, where he is unable to recognize himself. Even at his worst, when he is sprawled on the bathroom floor, he cannot avoid the mirror. Here, in Humphrey Davies' translation:

> In the bathroom, I curled up and vomited till my heart almost burst through my ribs. My pulse soon started to go down and remained terrifyingly slow. I had barely lifted my head to look at my reflection in the bathroom mirror when I blacked out and my eyes turned up to look at the ceiling lighting.

Not only is his reflection unrecognizable to him, but people in his immediate environment also start treating him harshly. K's family and

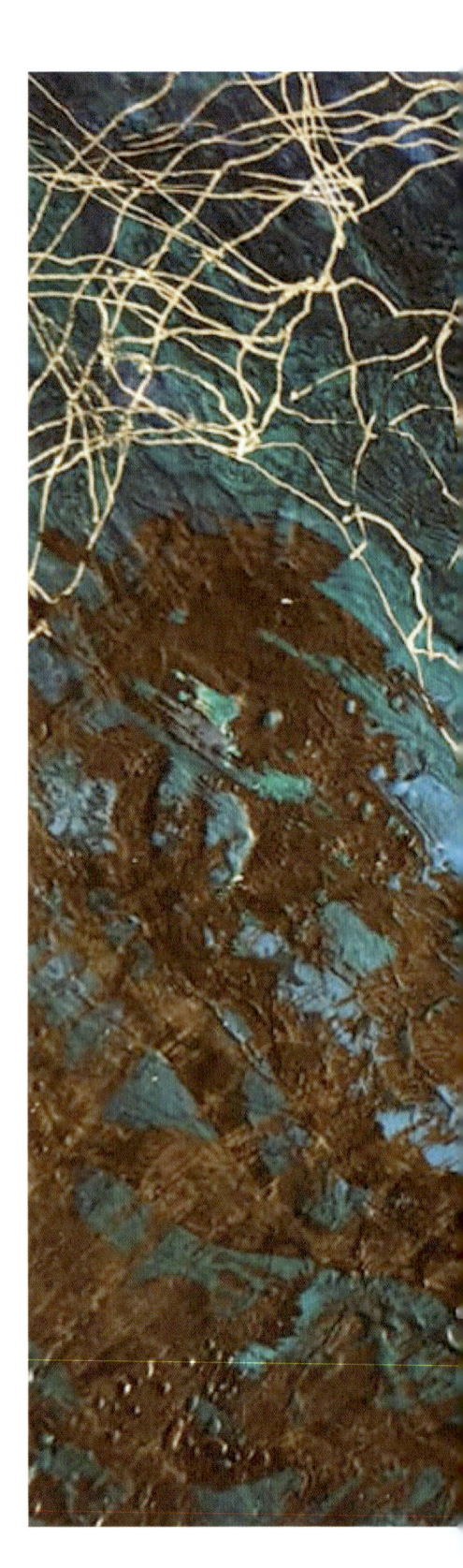

۲۱ / 21

friends constantly harass him with comments about his face, his weak body, his weight loss, and eventually they become the mirrors he needs to avoid. While this is a fictional narrative, comments also lurk in the archive of my memory:

> *"My darling, don't you ever use a mirror? A bit of blusher will help. Do you ever sleep?"*
>
> *"Have you looked in the mirror before? Why would I choose a girl like you?"*
>
> *"Here's a mirror, maybe if you fix a bit of that eyeliner, it'll help you look awake. At least for the picture."*

Each time I thought I looked "normal," I was reminded that perpetually sleepy eyes were not attractive, and even the sweetest women would tell me that makeup could fix every anomaly. Unsolicited advice came from every direction, as people were uncomfortable with the presence of a lacking female body. My first week of teaching, I walked to class, and before I knew it, someone had caught up with me to say hello. She was a lecturer I hadn't seen in ages, and she could hardly stop herself from commenting:

> "You walk strange. There's a limp. Or . . . it's like you're walking like a soldier. It's not a war, you can relax," she said jokingly.
>
> "Yes, there's a limp," I said.
>
> "It's like you're marching somewhere. Trying to scare the students, I suppose?"
>
> "No. See you!" I walked to my classroom, unable to shake the afterimage of her face.

I carried her face with me for the longest time, forgetting her name, forgetting the context of our conversation. It's easy to tell my students that beauty is in the eye of the beholder. It's easy to reiterate that women's bodies are conditioned to feel shame, that societal expectations are unfair, even cruel, and that we need to work our way through the shame to arrive at self-love. But the reality is that there are mirrors everywhere I look; even when I am doing my best to avoid them, they are there, unwelcome intrusions. There are voices that feel the need to reflect your image back to you, if only to urge you to reconsider who you are, how you navigate your world. It's easy to get rid of tiny, compact mirrors. It's harder to look away from a larger mirror, and impossible to avoid talking mirrors, glass that cuts at our deepest insecurities.

As always, I took my dilemma to my mother, who is an artist, and who has lots of mirrors in her studio. She was the first to speak to me about the beauty of broken mirrors, how they are more honest, how they don't believe in symmetry. When she looks at a mirror for too long, she claims the image changes. You either see too much or too little. You start getting used to a certain flaw, a missing detail, or you reconsider what you see.

"Break the mirror, then look. Hold anything up to a broken mirror, and you'll see a completely different image," she tells me, adding, "It's the same with brokenness in people. If you have a broken body, you won't need mirrors, as you'll have a broken mirror. Use it to look at society and yourself. It will change every day, it will keep cracking, and your vision will continue changing. There's nothing concrete, nothing perfect, *alkamal li Allah*."

My mother believes in art that is fragmented, and she never completes a painting without finding something in it to shatter, to tear apart. She will carve out pieces from a fully fleshed-out image so that she can break it, taking her cue from broken mirrors and the way they change our perception of images. Once the painting has parts of it removed, it starts to look more like "real art" to her. Its realness is in its lack. When I look at her paintings, especially the ones filled with intricate details of the spine and nerve fibers, I expect to see wholeness and completeness but am met with gaping holes. The image challenges my expectations of detail, wholeness in perfection, completeness in a carefully constructed image. There is nothing exact nor symmetrical about a broken image, and the challenge is adjusting my vision to accept its lack as beauty. Everywhere I look, people want complete and whole images, whole bodies, whole selves, and I still search for a self-image that makes sense to me. I am in a constant process of accepting what I see and avoiding talking mirrors that continue to cut.

Perhaps exactness and symmetry are what Plath was capturing, but perhaps she was missing the fact that broken mirrors will help us see wholeness in lack, and give us more to search for than symmetry ever will. Perhaps the narrator K needed a broken mirror but didn't know it. Perhaps I still search for brokenness in people, for vulnerability, and for a new self-image every day. All I know is that my mother's voice is the one talking mirror I carry with me as I navigate a reality filled with glass.

۲۳

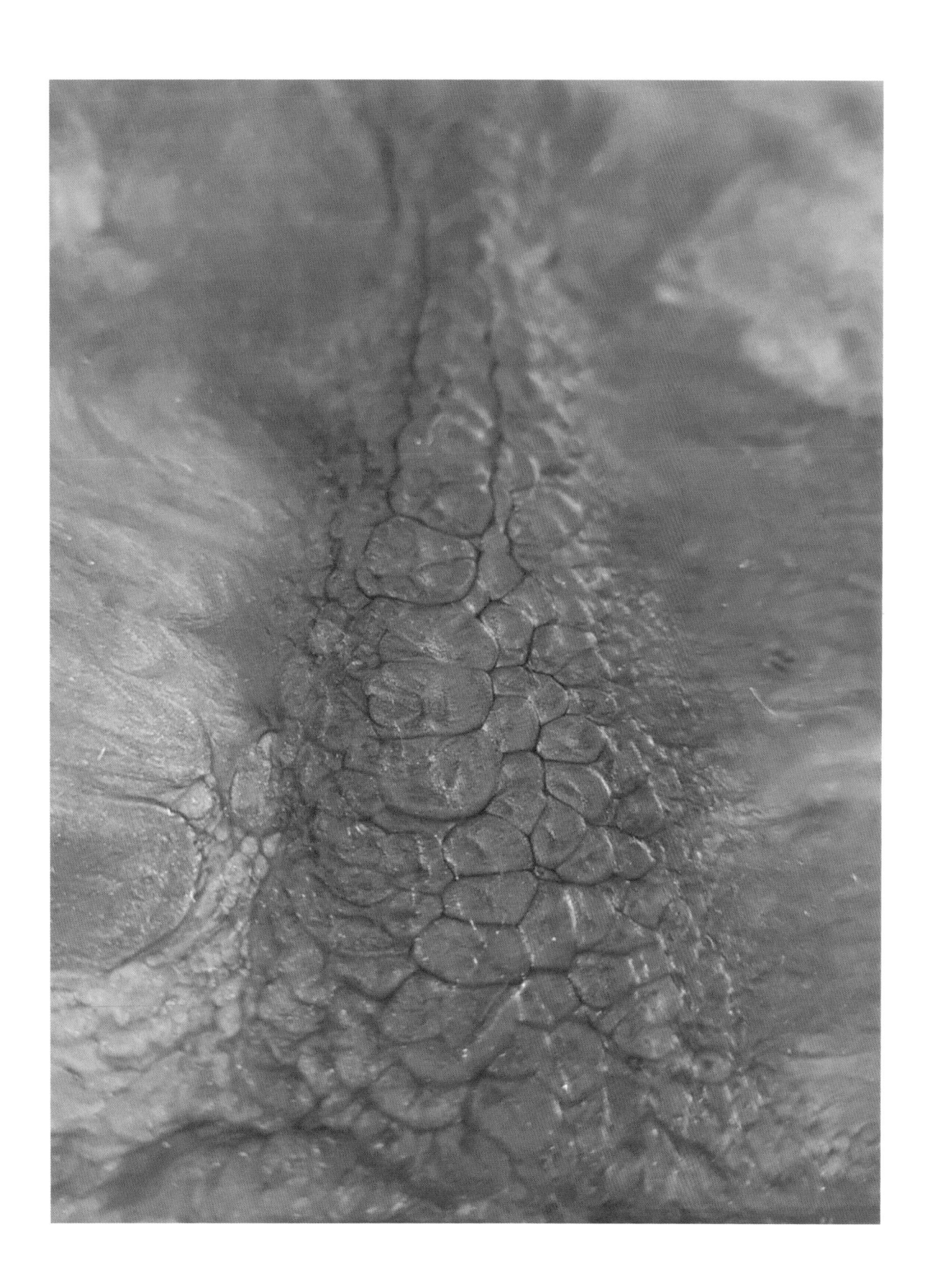

Poetry

On to the Next Room

By **Abdalrahman Alqalaq**

Translated by Sara Abou Rashed

Today, as you leave the tenth room,
you become obsessed with the origins
and meanings of things. You search
and ask around. For instance,
you ask a friend, "What is a *house*?"
"My house is my suitcase," he says.
He opens it and takes out a mirror and a watch.
Neither of you can bear the presence
of these two objects at once.
You ask him, "Then how did we meet?"
He says, "My *body* is my suitcase."
"What is a body?" you ask.
He leaves . . . and leaves your body waiting
for the bus, which you drag out
of your own wristwatch
and wish it had stopped working before this
and wish the road had lost its way to corners
and become a skyline——empty
of angles——a skyline laid out for you to roll
like your mother rolls winter rugs
then carries them
on to the next room——

Follow me,
my body, my road,
and the army of photos of loved ones
who will never again be the same:
on to the next room——

مقتطف من إلى الغرفة التالية

عبد الرحمن القلق

اليوم بينما تغادر الغرفة العاشرة
تصير مهووساً بأصول الأشياء ودلالتها
تبحث وتسأل من حولك
مثلاً
تسأل صديقك: ما البيت؟
فيقول: بيتي حقيبتي
ثم لا يقوى كلكيكما على بقاء الاثنين معاً
تسأله: كيف التقينا إذاً؟
يقول: بل جسدي حقيبتي
تسأله: ما الجسد؟
فيمضي... ويظل جسدك في انتظار الباص قبل ذلك
تخرجه من ساعة اليد
وتود لو أنها تعطلت قبل ذلك
وصار أفقاً بلا زوايا الطريق ضاعت من وجهة
ممتداً كأنك سجاد الشتاء
تحمله وتمضي إلى الغرفة التالية...

أيها الجسد، أيها الطريق
ويا جيش صور الأحبة الذين لن يعودوا مثلما كانوا
إلى الغرفة التالية...

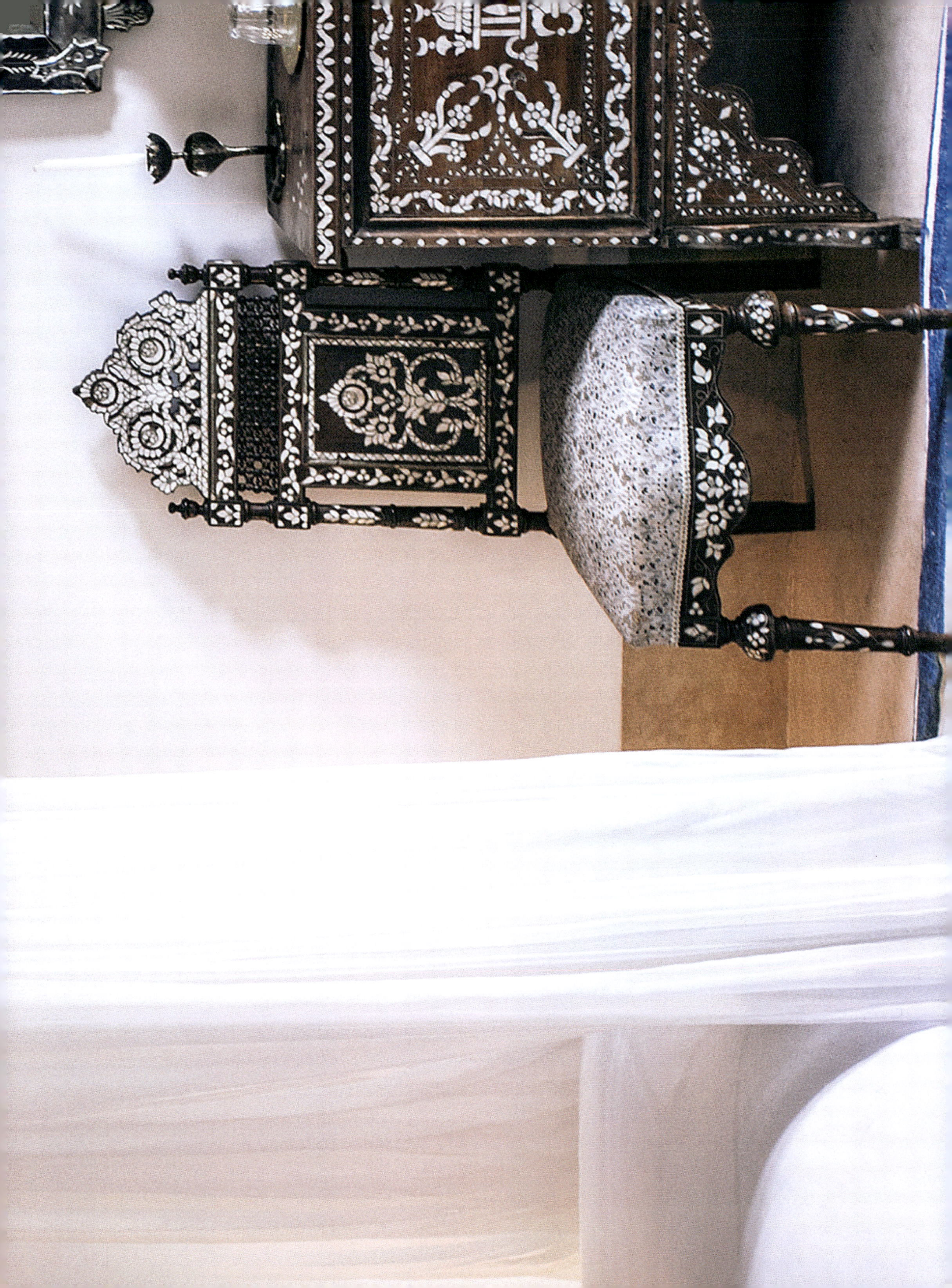

Excerpt

My Face Through the Seasons

By **Mohamed Choukri**

*We didn't have a mirror at home,
because none of us wanted to see his face in it.*

Translated by
Jonas Elbousty

۲۷ / 27

© WikiCommons, Pexels

In Tangier, my city of wonders, I get hit by a wave of depression whenever I fight with myself for no good reason. In the morning, I get depressed when I can't remember a beautiful dream to start out my day. I cling to dreams, because they are like Ariadne's thread in the city's labyrinth; they protect me from being soaked by the torrential rains of despair. I had a friend who believed that, if someone did not know how to dream, he should come to Tangier. That's the way it was. However, that same friend turned into an unbeliever, and so the city dragged him into its own particular hell. If the biggest dreamers fashion the world, then I've let my dream fashion its own world.

"When I forget the words, the images they form still remain." I feel disgusted whenever I discover that a person I considered a friend turns out to be an opportunist. I embalm him, placing him in one of the corners of my memory's cemetery, as a reminder of a part of my life.

I have discovered that a little excitement helps reanimate my heart, and a good deal of anger helps paralyze my body and scramble my thoughts. When I'm angry, my memory is useless.

My childhood is the darkest cloud in my life. No one ever rewarded what I was doing. I was just a child to be slapped. There wasn't even a single smile. I was living a life in which I could change nothing, because grown-ups were in control of everything. How will I ever be able to endure and confront what I went through as a child? My thoughts were caused neither by fear nor by bravery, but simply because I could not stop what was happening. I came to realize that a bitter life awaited me, so for a while I let it happen. In order to reward myself until that time came, I created my own childhood wonders. And if today I feel proud of being a witness to my own childhood, and the childhoods of others like me, it is because, in most of my writings, I do my best to unveil its darker moments. Everyone's life has its own clouds, some of them clear, others still hazy. Every childhood is like that. The village where I grew up has left no trace in my memory; it is just a distorted screen where pictures are projected: of myself, of others, and of misshaped forms. That childhood was destroyed by migration. I do not believe people who claim to know their entire childhood. They may have some vague feelings about it, but it is only a glimmer of light in a very dark space. It is impossible to know to what extent the author's childhood influences his own writing! He writes about his childhood from the perspective of a mature and grown adult. He circles around it because every childhood is hostage to its adulthood. The child during the "childhood phase" can be understood only by the child.

When the clouds of my life collide, my sleepy waiting mode is aroused. I believe in leading a life of emergencies. The clouds in my life urge me to grab whatever slips away from it. It is like a chip of flint: once it ignites, it becomes a spark, then a flame, and then turns into light.

I love mystery, quarrels, mirages, echoes, buds, the phoenix,

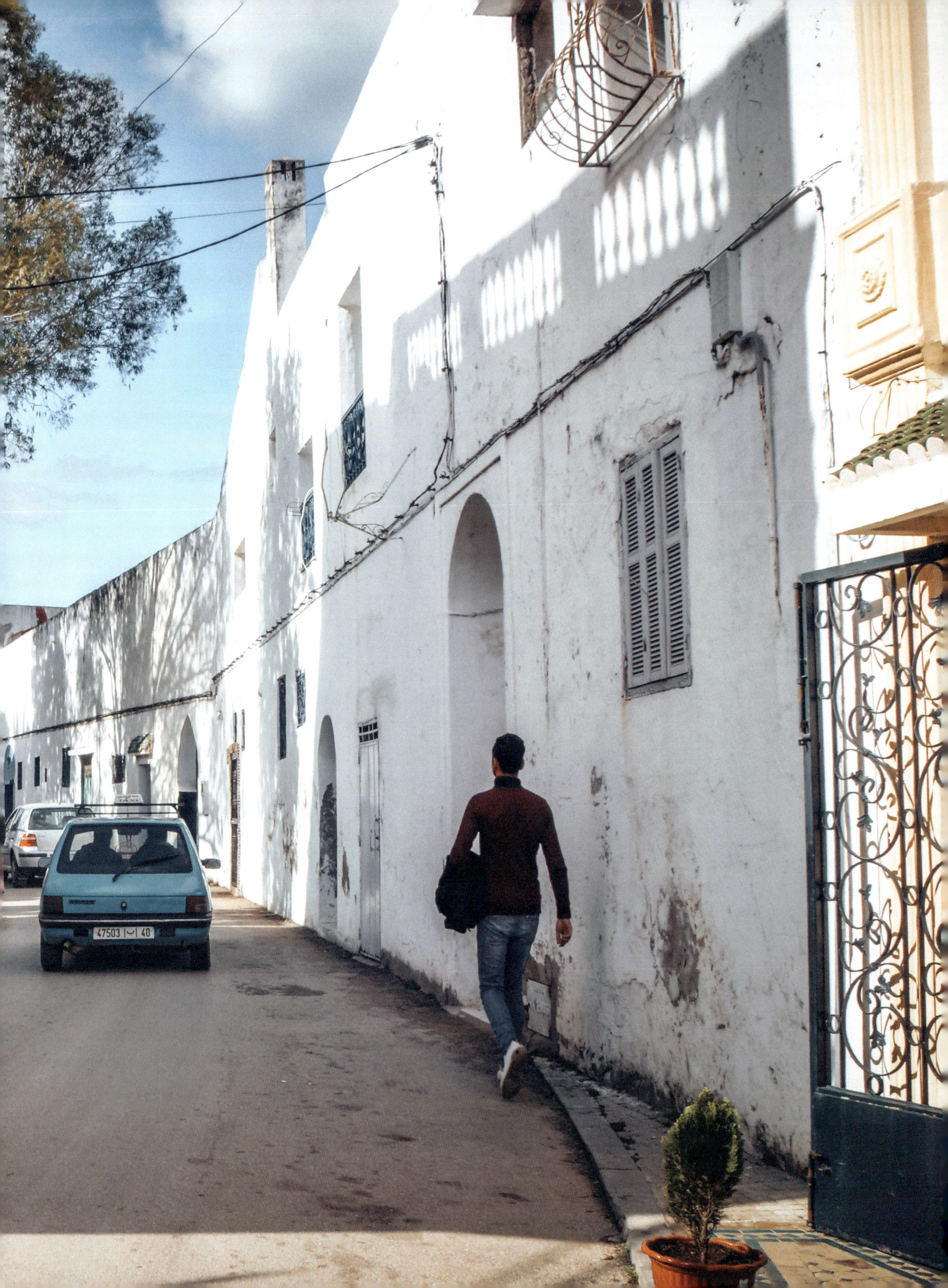

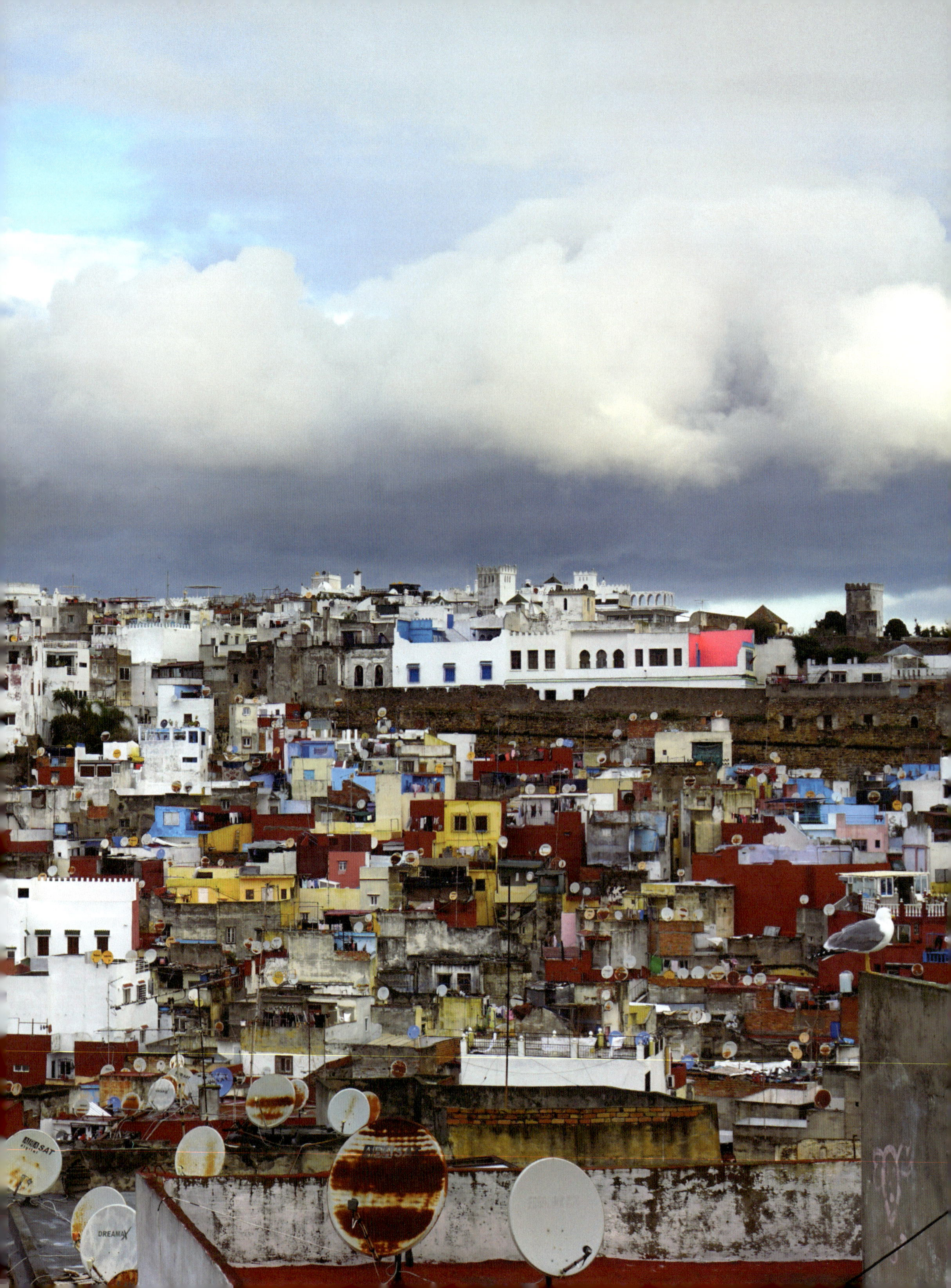
DREAMAX

the magic and fascination of ripples. *I am who I am*, and I long for creation's root to burst into bloom.

Whenever distress invades my life, I tap my reservoir of experiences to fight back. For my personal fortress, I have constructed a secret crypt; for my pyramid its locked exit; and for my tower its pathfinder telescope.

I am an Aries. I live between night and day. The wolf has the right to devour me, but I have the right to outsmart him and fight back.

My symbol will remain, but not my life.

In our present, we are always hard on the "past." It is like the grandmother we accuse of having dementia, forgetting that she was the one who shaped our imagination with her storytelling. If the past takes the form of the grandmother—the fountain of language—then the present is nothing but her grandson.

The coldness of my feelings is not like a seed that was born with me and which grew until it had deep, extensive roots. Whatever I have gained from my past experiences—traumas and seedlings that were planted here and there in the realm of my life—I have uprooted them all from their arboretum. The coldness of my feelings is only a temporary depression.

I was sitting alone in the Eldorado Restaurant when Laarbi el-Yacoubi passed by to remind me of his upcoming birthday. While waiting for his birthday, we had some champagne to celebrate my own. That is how I managed to overcome the worrisome aspects of turning sixty-four, with a moment of friendship.

Spring

Books and writing are the two sources that have never dried up, since first they burst into my life. They can suppress the normal sense of time and create a time that deepens creativity. They guide both my dreams and my gushing ideas. They free me from a narrow vision and lead me toward a broader perspective, an internal exile.

Our vision can only capture the entirety of space when in dreams. The ultimate goal: to make our own dreams come true before realizing the dreams of others.

The fountain of dreams never dries up if it reaches Don Quixote's level of madness. He moves from one dream to another, one conquest to another, until he grows feeble for a while. Victory does not matter to those obsessed by eternity. What would Don Quixote do with his life if he ever lost his madness? We might start by dreaming and end up completely mad. Don Quixote lived his entire life mad and died a sane person, as it is written on his grave . . . Hello . . . ! Who can be like him?

"The adventure is the only fountain from which I filch fleeting happiness."

I harvested my first win when I dedicated myself to reading and writing; then I rid myself of the curse of my official job, with all its boasting bosses and employees who kissed the asses up the hierarchy in hope of promotion. Now, I can get intoxicated on my own nectar. I have preferred to be alone and to work for my own profit, whether I have won or lost. I have let creativity well up from existence and nothingness, from fullness and void, from futility and counteraction to the higher cause.

The creative person is someone who instills in me the seedling of effusion and transcendence, someone who can plant words and use them to shape visions and imaginations. I do not believe in hope that is devoid of my own ambitions and hard work. Hope alone engenders procrastination and distraction. Only a child has the right to hope. Indeed, a child can't change a thing. If it does happen, then it has to be a miracle, or coincidence.

Nature's guitar plucks at the strings of my heart when I am inside its heart, and it is there when I talk to it. The Nature created by our imagination is more beautiful than nature itself. When I am far removed from it, I feel deeply intoxicated by its winds and sounds. Nature is what shapes our manners. It is from Nature that we derive the things that encourage us when we are sad; it is our refuge when we lose our rapport with the nature of humans.

The most beautiful flower in my life is wild. Its scent disappears when one approaches it; it withers when one sows it. It grows and gives off scent only when it is in its own volcanic clay. Its name is carved in its arbor, and it vanishes when it goes back to its ashy eternity. Every time it is resurrected, it adopts a different color, just like a chameleon. It uses its poisonous nectar to protect its virginity so that no one can pick it and stop the pollen from wafting far away. Call it the Goddess of Flowers, if you will, for it does not have a name.

I'll donate the rest of my life to anyone who can use it to enlighten people's vision within the tunnel of their thought. I don't care so much about people's identities as I care about their effectiveness. I realize that my life's bouquet will be very thorny. I should hand it only to someone with a callous hand, leaving it to whoever wants it.

The word "success" reminds me of a theatrical smile or a sneaky business deal. I do not like to cram myself into an auction, bidding for the word "success," because it violates my ambition.

Summer

It was unbearably hot waiting for the unknown. Many things happened, but what we wished would happen never did. I lost as much as I won. I didn't gamble with everything I had. There are paradises I've heard about. I was eager to see them, but I changed my mind. Today, I do not crave "a garden, high and fertile: heavy rain falls on it but makes it yield a double increase of harvest" (Quran, 2:265). Yearning robs me of life's pleasures.

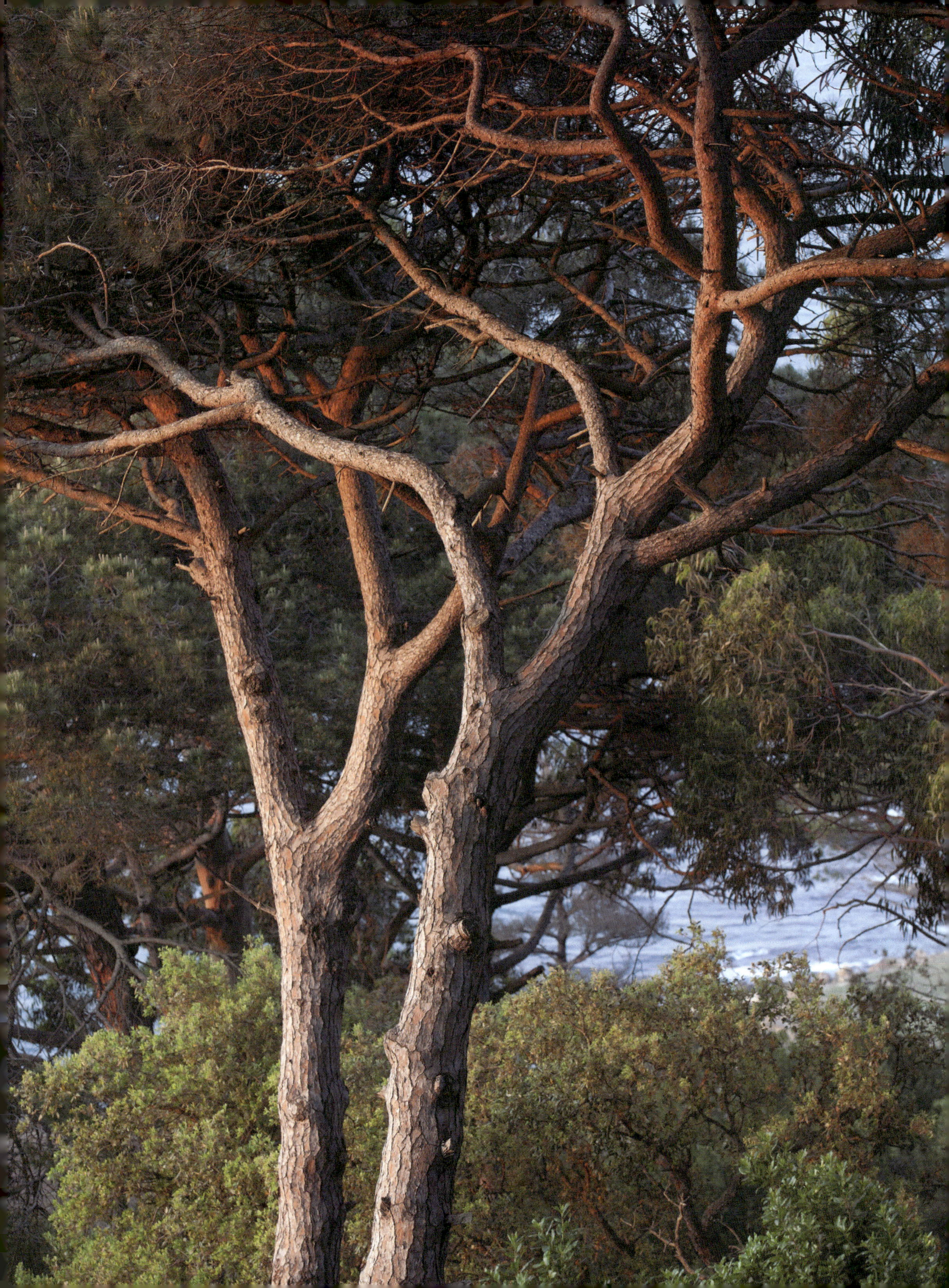

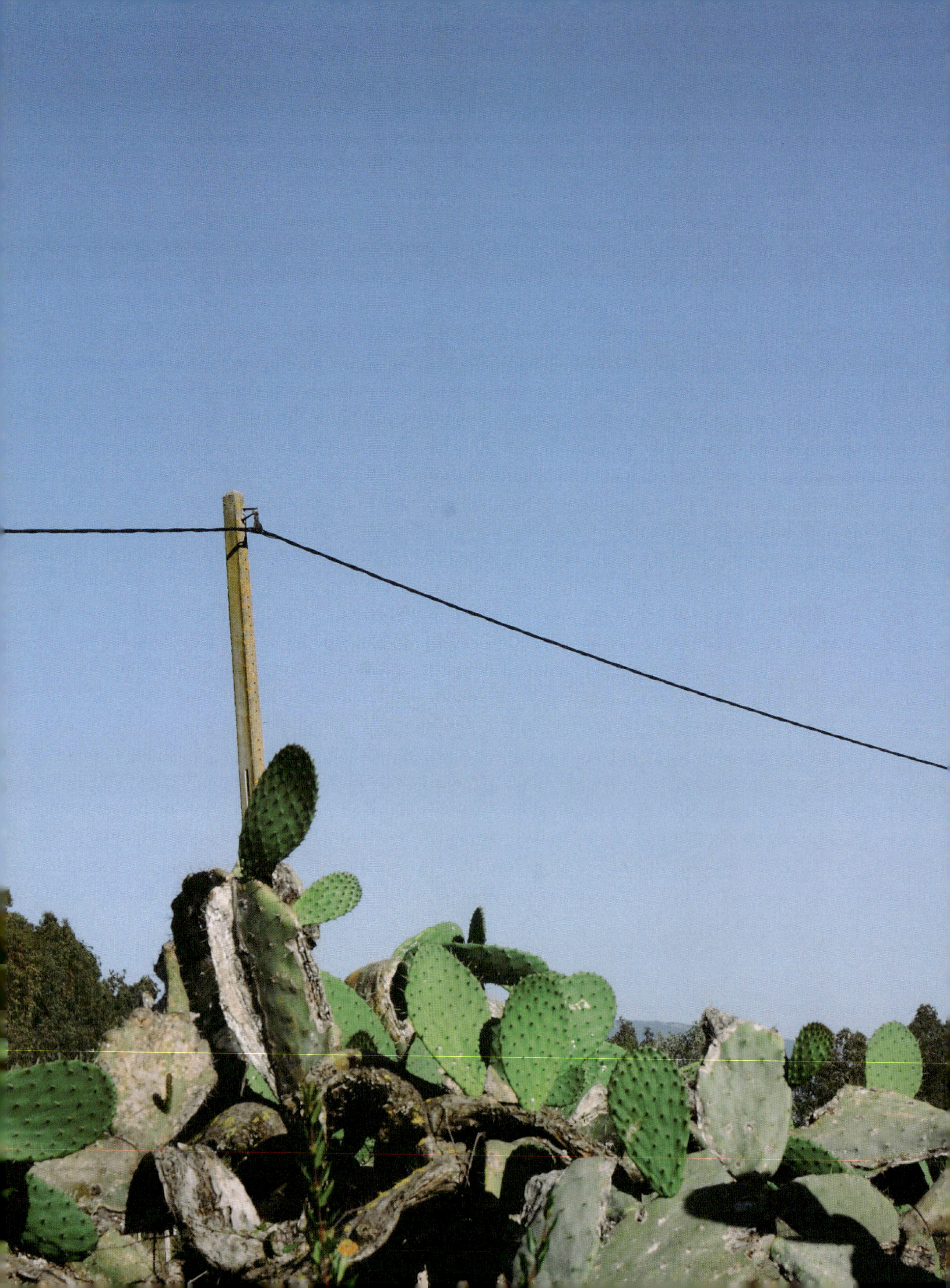

Too much honesty is a folly that leads only to recklessness. I might well be scorched by a madness that unleashes joy and awakens the delights of beauty. The image only excites me in that it manages to inspire the creation of the image dwindling inside it.

Absolute frankness is a death penalty to every possibility of agreement.

When I honestly confess what I know about people and other things, I create an enemy that, unknown to me, might take revenge on me even in my own imagination.

Honesty is not always the ultimate truth. What keeps me tied to some reality is the joyful idea that I create about it and the temptations with which it can challenge me.

The thing I relish about the crush of life is the amount I can gather from its scattered fragments. I do not expect someone to make me happy; I'm the one to make myself happy, according to my mood.

At the site of wild beauty, I never touch. I only toy with what is hidden. Ostentation is allowable for the impotent, but, as the traditional tale has it, there's no buttermilk for every Dakhtanūs in summer.

The cold breeze that refreshes me is the one that takes me by surprise, just like summer rain.

A little bit of hatred gets the blood flowing, stretches the arteries, and gets the heart pumping again. However, a lot of hatred blows everything apart. The same applies to paranoia: a little might help one to be creative, but a lot results only in delusion and schizophrenia.

If I have an important appointment with someone I hate, I yell loud insults at him in my own bathroom. As a result, when I meet him, I do not feel the need to insult him twice, whether out loud or in secret.

I hate those who stop me from writing. The only way I know of making peace with them is through writing, which always wins out against prohibition.

I feel how sweet life is when I wake up and distribute my morning gazes from my balcony, like an eagle soaring ever higher. I can discern everything in sight: everything I can recall from my happy memory, or everything I have dreamed. I can recall enjoying that first sip from a vintage wine, what music I listened to, and how it reminded me of the woman I used to love. She would knock on my door, but my desire for a dreamy solitude would win out over human temptation.

Whenever I have all or part of this at my disposal, I feel the softness of life, as the scrapping cats inside my head calm down and submit. I'm served any iced drink by my mother, a female friend, or the woman I have just met. I am cautious about what lovers serve me, even if it comes from their mouths; I'm careful even of my own sisters.

I do not necessarily drink my iced drink during a heatwave. I savor it by taking in sips, not gulps. The wild grapes may come from a fox, a bear, a snake, or a colocynth.

Autumn

A person may shed his leaves when he dries up; he may get them back if his roots run deep, and if his water-table is not drained. Leaves are not the same in the way they fall, change color, and fade. As every leaf falls, it has its own immunity and role—or it may be broken off before it matures. It is well known that everything that grows and has leaves is fated to decay.

I only acknowledge autumn years when I feel completely incapable of doing things that I could easily do before. Death may well catch us first. No one can guarantee the fruits in his paradise.

In the autumn years, humans can either be wise or senile, either picker or picked.

Sweet things taste bitter to me, and bitter things sweet.

I am no longer tempted by all those fancy feasts unless they are plain and simple. I no longer sigh over what I once had and let slip, whether willingly or not. I remember everything, and do not. I do not cling to a fragile branch even though it is dripping with honey. I face life's pallor with a blend of yellow, blue, and white until I get my proper color. I was never overcome by a life of austerity. I remain in touch with life, but do not confront its stormy waves. Whenever I set sail at the right time, I usually reach my destination.

There is no such person as a victorious hero or a defeated one All heroism involves servitude. I am my own servant. To me, ambition is synonymous with achievement in every excess of stupidity.

Leaves are not alike in the way they fall, nor are dreams. Some dreams are strong, others weak, transparent, foggy, joyful, or scary. We do not choose our dreams, and yet they are closely connected with our consciousness and subconsciousness. Many of our dreams reveal secrets of a past or future life. Our dreams are our fate, whether we accept or reject their magic. Dreams can often enlighten a dark side of our life and inspire us to reach our goals. When I stop dreaming, I resort to daydreams, though they are not as strong as real dreams, which hold the keys to our secret life. My face is my magical dreams.

I do not care how many leaves drop from my own autumn tree. It has already offered its color, fruits, taste, and nectar. Everything has happened, whether I liked it or not. Of my sorrows, all I can recall are things that soften their roughness and urge me to remember their more pleasant aspects. We should not always define ourselves by how we end or how we start; things may end the way they start, or start the way they end. We are who we become!

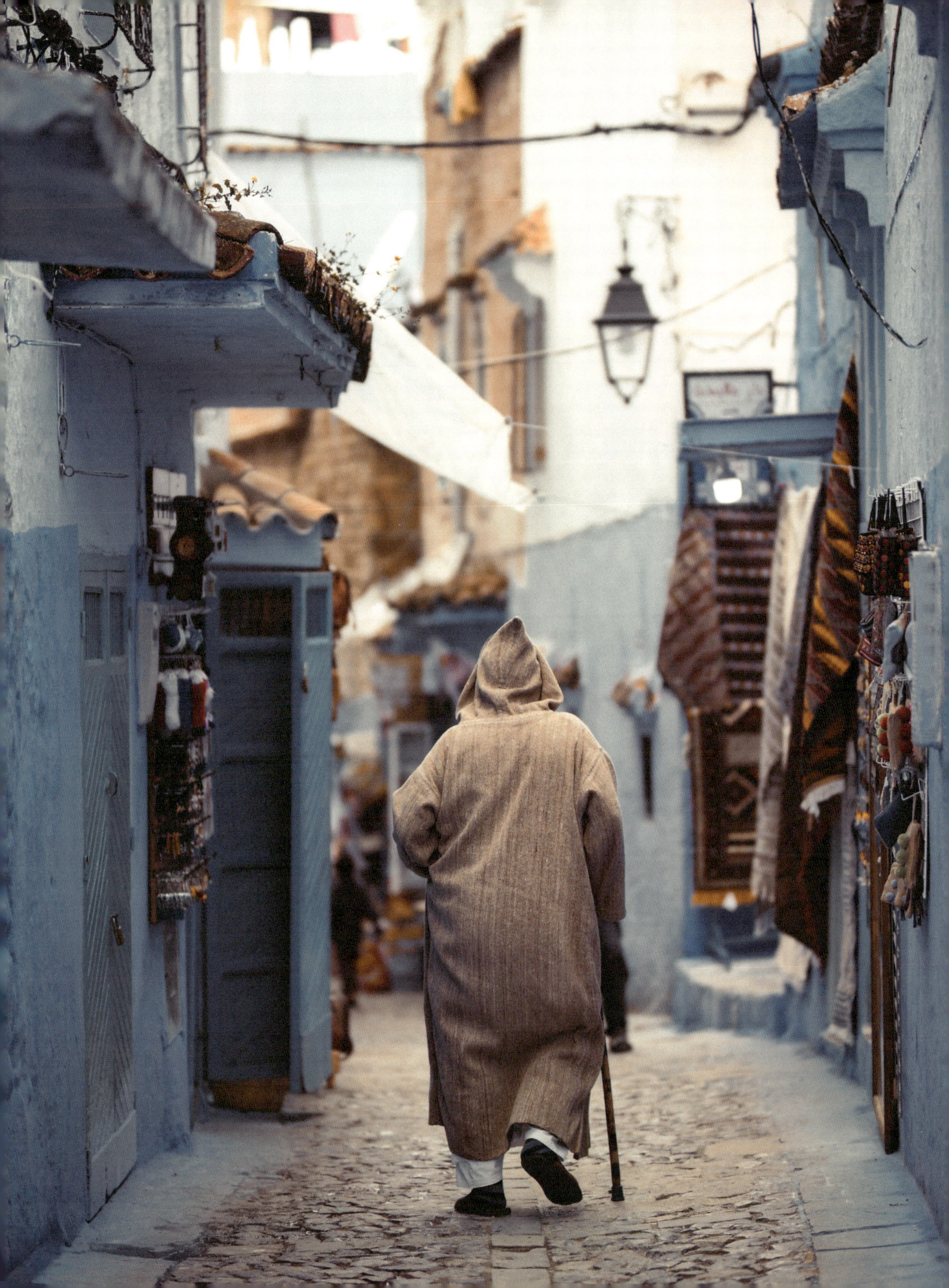

Poetry

Reflection

By Rym Jalil

Translated by Nawara Belal

Oh mother
the insides of your womb
had an encapsulating glittery darkness
and a ceiling of enlightenment

…

The sea carries its own story:
I was shunned by the wave that retreated from me
and, even before you called for me
I ran, in a frenzy

…

Once I learned to float
I called on the creatures
in silence:
The octopus came,
the owl
and the squid, seeing me perplexed,
turned to stone.
He glimpsed in me a sense
of the pain humans can inflict
and wished himself a snake

…

And one Cairiene night
with only me and my imaginary worldings,
a guava tree and the two kittens,
the owl closed in on me and flared its wings
in, one could say, a state of conflict,
or rather: an introvert acting of its own volition,
even in wholesome coyness

…

يا بآ بآمي
جوه رحمك كان فيه خلقة بتلمع
وكان فيه سقف بنور

…

أما البحر حكايته حكاية
بعدت عني كل موجة
وقبل حتى ما تنبئيني
جريت في حالة هوجة

…

لما اتعلمت أطفو
نديت على الكائنات
في صمت:
جاني أخطبوط
جاني بومة
فاتحول صخرة
شاف فيا ذكرى
عن أذى الإنسان أو كان تعبان

…

وفي ليلة نديت من ليالي القاهرة
مكانش فيه غير أنا و في خيالي
شجرة جوافة والقطتين
قربت مني وفردت جناحيها
تقدر تقول حالة جدال
أو كان انطوائي بيظهر على وقته
بالرغم من الخجل

…

Ohh mama,
if you could see the sea
become a mirror.
Come, let me tell you my story.
Your fear has taken over my imagination
and my reflections haven't been of my own making.
Your drowned ship sank inside me,
but
I have only just
found someone
to stand beside me.

يا ماما
شفتي البحر
طلع مراية
تعالي أحكيلك حكاية
خوفك تغلغل خيالي
وانعكساتي مكانتش على هوايا
مركبك الغرقان عاش جوايا
وأنا بدوبك لقيت حد يقف معايا

Simon Berger © Pexels

Jordan

Sad Woman's Mirrors

By **Maheera Migdadi**

T She takes her time peeling the heavy blanket from her cold body. Grudgingly, she slides out of bed and drags herself to the bathroom. She wipes her hand over the mirror like she's waving goodbye; her drowsy face looks back at her from the blurry glass, reminding her of all the hours she hasn't slept. It warns of the long day ahead. She'll be holding her breath for the next twenty-four hours.

Translated by
Madeline Edwards

13/41

Footsteps dragging, body slumped over. There are plenty of taxis, but none will take her. And despite all the years she's been working, she doesn't own her own car, or apartment, or even a little cat.

She has no choice but the bus, a means of automatic transport between the stop that's far from her house (which she gets to on foot) and the stop that's also far from her work. Every day shuffles between walking and bus riding.

Most days she claims the seat where she can see the world behind her, through the bus driver's side-view mirror. The world is always slipping away, and she alone is moving forward. She knows deep down that the entire world is moving forward, while she is the only one leaving, endlessly falling backward. There is no ultimate destination for her falling, no stops along the way, no quick break along the side of the road.

In the elevator, she stands in front of the mirror. How frumpy she looks! She imagines that if she moved, she'd ripple and sway like an empty dress on a clothesline, struck by wind on all sides. So she stays like this for the whole ride, glued in place, so no one can discover her emptinesses.

In the office, she looks at the image reflected in her computer screen. Not much different from yesterday or the day before yesterday. If it wasn't for the lines around her eyes, which have increased by two, and the sagging cheeks that seem to have sagged further, she'd swear that when she leaves the office at the end of each day the image of her face stays there, fixed on the dormant computer's screen. In the street, at the end of the day, a very long day, you see her completely exhausted, reflected in the puddle left behind by a cloud the sun failed to notice.

This time, she stops, contemplates the puddle, asks: "In this entire universe, isn't there one mirror, one shiny reflective thing, that makes me look pretty?"

She taps the puddle with her toe. Soft, gentle waves ripple through her reflection.

It dissipates, a candle in a moment's breeze, flavoring it like an end without closure. She sheds a tear that hits the sidewalk, and she knows her reflection now sits firmly on its surface, but she refuses to look. Instead, she raises her eyes and sees a peddler carrying mirrors with all sorts of shapes, sizes, and decorations.

"Sayyidati, would you like to buy a mirror?"

"What do I need a mirror for, when I'm the mirror of so many sad women?"

She leaves and keeps leaving, no stops along the way.

HIGHLIGHTS *from*
THE LIBRARY OF ARABIC LITERATURE

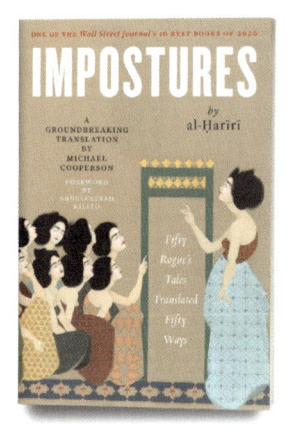

"An important translation of a criminally neglected work of world literature."
—*Mada Masr*

Impostures
by al-Ḥarīrī
Translated by Michael Cooperson
Foreword by Abdelfattah Kilito

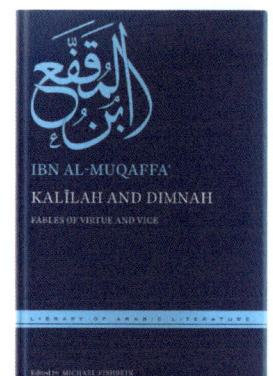

A mirror for princes, with timeless fables of loyalty and betrayal

Kalīlah and Dimnah
Fables of Virtue and Vice
by Ibn al-Muqaffaʿ
Edited by Michael Fishbein
Translated by Michael Fishbein and James E. Montgomery

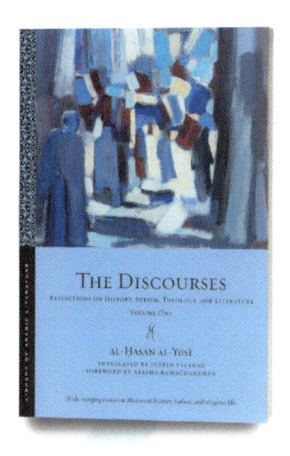

Essays on Moroccan history, Sufism, and literature

The Discourses
Reflections on History, Sufism, Theology, and Literature
Volume One
by al-Ḥasan al-Yūsī
Translated by Justin Stearns
Foreword by Ayesha Ramachandran

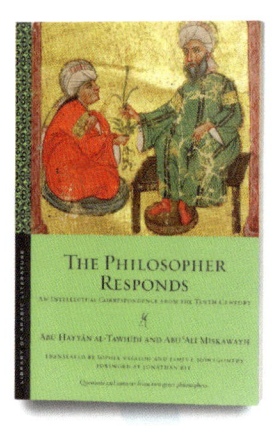

"A fascinating read, particularly for the aspiring scholar of classical Arabic texts."
— *Al Jadid*

The Philosopher Responds
An Intellectual Correspondence from the Tenth Century
by Abū Ḥayyān al-Tawḥīdī and Abū ʿAlī Miskawayh
Translated by Sophia Vasalou and James E. Montgomery
Foreword by Jonathan Rée

Available online or at your local bookstore
WWW.LIBRARYOFARABICLITERATURE.ORG
WWW.NYUPRESS.ORG
WWW.COMBINEDACADEMIC.CO.UK (UK/EUROPE)

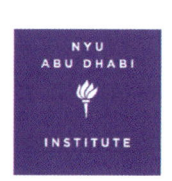

Jordan

Glass

By **Rema Hmoud**

Translated by
Ibrahim Fawzy

All the cups are arranged neatly on the middle shelf of the glass cupboard that occupies a corner of the hall, near the see-through dining table with its burgundy chairs. A large deep dish made of black glass, filled with colorless glass fruits, sits in the middle of the hall.

The colossal windows, which look out over worrisome spaces, are covered with sheer curtains embroidered with fine gold threads. Under a big, skinny, wide-screen TV, there is a black cabinet with glass and a lot of nonsense antiques.

And I . . . I hate the glass. It makes me nervous, needling me with its stupidity as it reflects my image whenever I pass by. It sees me as too tall or too wide, with a mouth as big as a plate and eyes that are set too far from my mouth, so I hurry away, only to find the glass mocking me from the TV cabinet, or above my head when I'm washing dishes, or in the metal sheen on the oven or fridge.

I neglect the glass until the dust makes it change color, and oil or water stains take over the kitchen, covering most of the glass until its ability to irritate me gradually abates. Only when I know that one of my friends is coming over do I pick up the blue rag that's just for glass, and the washer fluid, and I spray every last piece in a temper to remove the dust, then wipe it slowly, for fear that it will break, and the glass beneath it shatter.

For days, I suffer these strange prolongations of my physiognomy, and this usually drives me to take shelter in a bedroom that has a huge mirror at its center. I sometimes cover the bedroom mirror, so as not to see my reflection. Then, I feel like being alone by myself. I talk to myself, comfort myself, and dust it carefully and gently. I put it back into its worn-out mold. I lock it up with a smile and leave my isolation humbled, time and again.

Once, when I welcomed one of my friends, she came in wearing her shoes, stepped on my new carpet, and sat on the big sofa. Like a bear with a sore head, she removed the embroidered pad from the sofa and threw it on the ground. I tried to hide the grimace that nearly floated over the surface of my face. We started our chat and she frequently moved her hand.

Under the TV, I looked at the glass, where I saw my reflection, tall and deformed as usual. I noticed her reflection, and it was the same as she really was, with no difference at all—extended neither in length nor width. I became nervous, and my right leg began to shake. I moved off the sofa and turned my back on the case and the TV. But I felt my reflection standing behind me, so elongated that I could see its shadow extending in front of me and covering her. Then, it shortened and stretched out horizontally. I saw it under and beside me while she sat with a novile, indecent reflection like mine.

In her presence, the air was sticky; I couldn't control my anger, which appeared sporadically on my face with a silly smile. I felt a terrible need to cut my hand with a knife made of air and stain all the glass with my blood. Only then might it calm down.

When I served the two glasses of juice, it spilled and splashed onto me. I bent to rub the stains off my dress, but then I saw the too-broad reflection of my nose in the tiled floor that I had mopped so carefully before her arrival. Her reflection sat quiet and normal.

Before she left, I was about to suffocate. I quietly closed the door after her, cursed everything around me, searched for air, and caught it with difficulty. All the glass in the space was gazing at me like a black hole, biding its time before it swallowed me without warning. How much I hate being watched! I lifted my dress from the cold floor, brought out big cardboard boxes I'd hid behind the case, and collected all the existing glass. With violent anger, I yanked the glass doors from their cases and buried all the glass in boxes. I reveled in the sound of glass being smashed on the street while I stood on the balcony.

Egypt

Closer than They Appear

By **Enas Eltorky**

Translated by the author

The door was ajar, and the mirror hanging above it announced the seer, who was inside. In the past, the door had remained shut to the long line of people waiting in front of it. It would open for a moment to let in the person whose turn had come, before firmly shutting once again. But now, there were no longer any lines, and no endless crowds fighting to step forward and enter. The place was quiet, except for the whistle of the wind and the creak of the door, which moved from time to time. The mirror hung from one end, while the opposite was left dangling. Its edge was broken, and it was covered in a thick dust that had accumulated over the years she had spent in the labyrinth of exile into which she had fallen. Still, it served as clear identification of the woman who dwelled inside.

She was a unique seer. She didn't have a crystal ball in which to read the future, nor did she hold the palms of her visitors to read their fortunes. Instead of a crystal ball, her face was a clear mirror, in which her visitors could see the reflections of their innermost souls. Rather than reading their palms, it was her visitors who would take her hand, playing their own tunes on it. She had long, graceful, pointed fingers. Whoever took hold of them was able to play them like the keys of a piano, or raise them to his lips like a woodwind or brass instrument. If the visitor spread her fingers a little bit, it was also possible to play them like a stringed instrument. They would play, and the tunes of their souls' melodies would reverberate. These could only be heard through her fingers. However, after all that happened—and after she had been banished to her exile—only the extremely brave, or the extremely desperate, attempted to pay her a visit.

Back in the days when she held her place in the middle of the playing field known as the city, the commotion outside her door didn't betray the silence behind it. The face of the mirror was as calm as a lake, waiting for them to throw the stones of their souls into its depths, and to read their innermost depths in what appeared on its surface. Her fingers lay spread in front of her, waiting for someone to question them. Everyone outside had their heads off their shoulders, and the roads were crowded with heads rolling like footballs, kicked by their owners in an attempt to score a goal in the nets of their opponents. A person would kick their head up high, hoping for their shot to be true, so that their head would rest on the shoulders of their opponent. Then they would jump with joy, rejoicing in this success in imposing their mind on another, on fixing it to someone else's shoulders—indifferent to the fact that they had become headless. They simply continued running, so that someone else wouldn't have the chance to outwit them with a shot that pinned another head on their neck. Only those who stood in line at her door kept their heads, so that they could face her mirror when it was their turn to enter. In spite of all this, it was possible to glimpse one of them, every now and then, leaving their place in the line to take part in the ongoing matches, before returning once again. Petty arguments and fights would erupt over whose turn it was, sometimes escalating so much that someone might kick someone else's head off their shoulders, so that it rolled away.

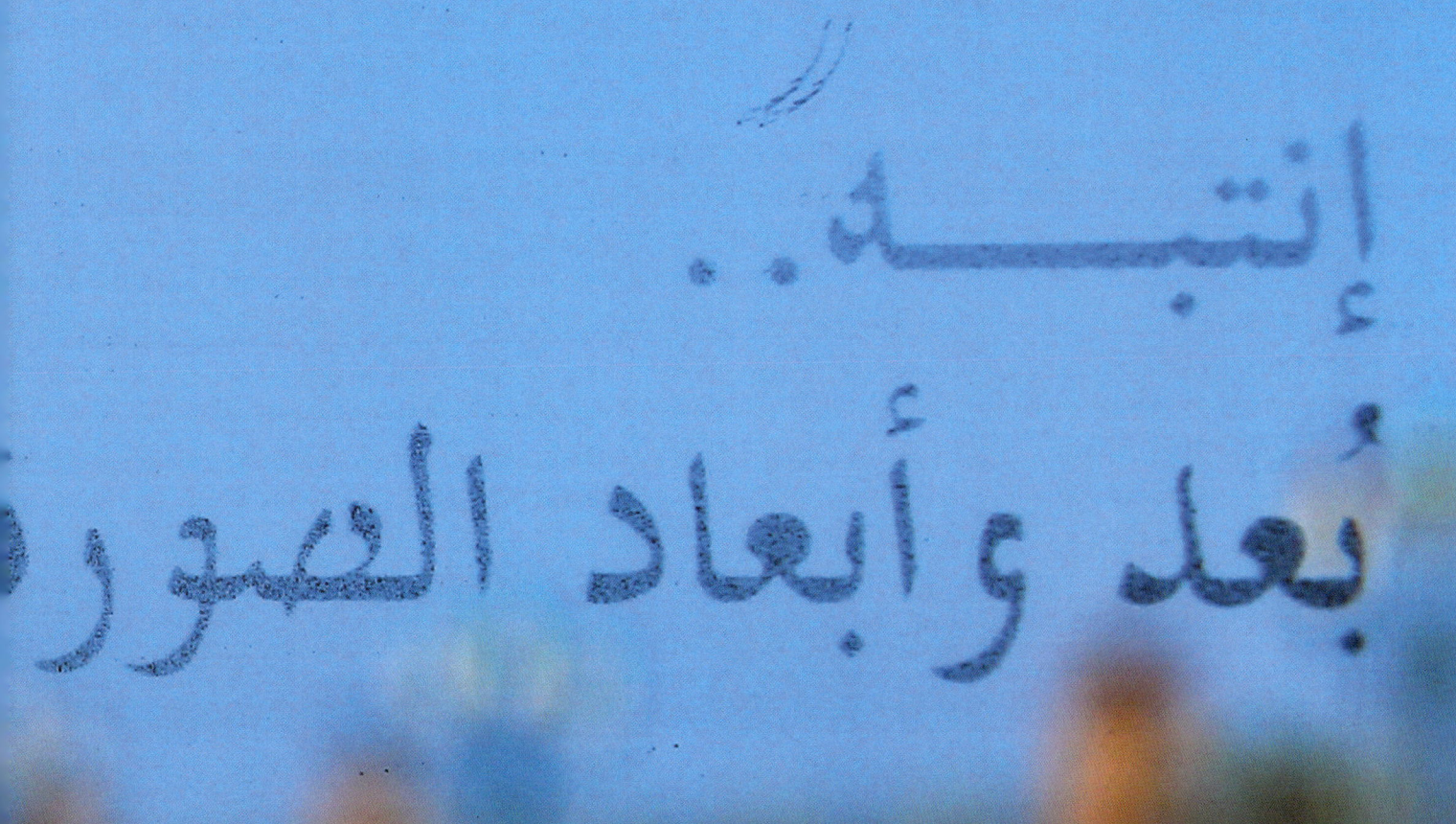

Behind the door, her head, with its clear mirror in front, was lined from the inside with a thick layer of lead. This covered the back of the mirror, preventing any of the visions reflected on its surface from seeping into her soul. Her heart, too, was a lead safe, as an additional line of defense, with a secure lock, whose secret combination was unknown to anyone, just as no one knew what was hidden inside it. Despite the large number of people who passed through her door, no one ever heard her voice, except for one phrase she directed to everyone who entered her mirror: "Objects in the mirror are closer than they appear." No one had ever understood the exact meaning of the words, but the wise among them interpreted them as meaning that whosoever crossed the threshold of that door, even though they may desire to see the truth reflected in the mirror, might not be able to fully face the whole truth. What they saw was merely a miniature reflection, a bit farther away than it actually was in reality.

Their inability to understand her words never stood as a barrier between her door and those waiting in front of it, lining up and fighting to enter. One entered carrying on his shoulders a head in the shape of an antique chest, securely shut with tight locks, giving the impression that its contents were among the most rare and precious treasures. Facing her mirror, he saw a coffin, worms crawling out of the gaps in its rotting wood. His fingers played the long fingers extended in front of him, which emitted rusty sounds as they clanged noisily against one another, along with the beats of hollow drums. Another entered, carrying a head in the shape of an intricately braided loaf, sprinkled with golden sesame seeds, with tiny white flowers blooming amidst its crevices. She sat facing the mirror, and her features were revealed as a black apple intertwined with thorns and a writhing snake with venom dripping from its fangs. The graceful fingers raised to her lips emitted a faint hiss that rose to a howling storm. Among all those who exited the seer's door, none uttered a word to those waiting outside, none telling of what they had seen within or helping them to interpret the meaning of her words.

One morning, the city, which had always been occupied with head games, woke to find that a single idea had settled within all the heads without exception: whether it was those rolling along the roads; or those suspended in the air, hunting for some goal to land upon, fixing themselves to some neck or the other; or even those that rested on their own shoulders, or upon the shoulders of others by force. Everyone stopped suddenly, and a silent hush prevailed throughout the city. The rolling heads stopped, some with their faces stuck in the dirt, while the flying heads were frozen mid-air, and remained suspended in space. There was no longer any point in exchanging heads, or trying to impose one's head on others, since all heads had become equal, containing the same idea. The idea had crept out from behind the seer's door, and spread with those who exited that door after facing the mirror. The crowd roared in unison, a single thundering shout, as they besieged her door: "Show us the naked Truth!"

The universe froze for a moment, and the flow of time stopped. Then the door quietly opened. The mirror faced them, its surface gleaming under the sun. Thousands of distorted overlapping images were reflected before their eyes, rivaling their darkest, most terrifying nightmares. Once again, she repeated her words clearly for them to hear: "Objects in the mirror are closer than they appear." For the first time ever, her words seeped deep inside them, the intended meaning shining in their minds. Their reality that they saw reflected in her mirror grew closer to them than their jugular veins. All those who had refused to acknowledge their reflection in the mirror found that what they had previously seen had become their visible reality. And all those who cried out, demanding to see the naked Truth, found that what rested upon their shoulders—and within their hearts and souls—had become the exact same as what they'd seen reflected in the mirror. Their shapes and images matched those reflected in the mirror, after the masks had fallen. They were stuck to their reality, with no hope of escape. They understood the seer's warning too late, after the curse had settled upon them.

Speech disappeared, and protesting cries and howls rose up instead. Some hurled stones at the face of the mirror, and others struck the shiny surface with their newly sprouted hooves. The mirror cracked, its face splintering into dozens of small irregular segments. In each segment, the same images were repeatedly reflected, multiplying their nightmares before their eyes, multiplying the terror. They chased her, driving her out of the cursed city. Whoever wanted to face the mirror now had to descend into the pitch-black belly of a deep valley. There ghosts and phantoms wrestled, giving out deafening, terrifying screams. If a person succeeded in making it out of the valley's depths alive, they would then have to climb a mountain, the top of which no eye could glimpse. The sun settled at its summit, dazzling and scorchingly hot. Whoever crossed the top of the mountain and passed between the rays of the sun, simply had to lie down upon the surface of a river that would carry him to the foot of the mountain, where he would find a dirt road, leading to the seer's cottage at its end.

Far away, in the streets of the city, a little girl gathered up the remains, picking up whatever heads caught her fancy among those lying at the sides of the road without anyone to claim them. She picked out specific details from all those features, carefully dusting them off and wiping them with her hands before putting them in the patched-up bag tied around her waist. At the end of each day, she sat by herself in a corner of some wasteland, her legs stretched out in front of her, and emptied the contents of her bag beside her, turning the heads over in her hands, searching for what she wanted. She selected a piece, studied it closely, before removing part of her own face and casting it aside, in order to replace it with the new piece. After, she would lay down to sleep on her side, placing her palm between her cheek and the dirt. She formed her features from the remains of the cursed city, and her face resembled a mosaic of recycled scraps. She intended to make the journey in the morning: down the valley, up the mountain top, and across the river, until she reached the door above which the mirror hung.

As she started her journey through the city streets, she was accompanied by curses and showered with insults and obscenities. All who saw her bid her farewell with gobs of spit that she simply wiped away, calmly, before she continued on her way with her eyes fixed on the horizon. She was followed by their death wishes: both for herself and for the woman whom she was risking everything to reach. Curses showered on the head of anyone who dared to contemplate contacting the seer, who was the cause of their curse and affliction. However, revenge was multiplied this time, because they were stronger than a little girl who had spent her days in the streets and slept in the corner of a wasteland. That's all they needed; a little girl who constructed her features from the remnants of their own, and who had no known mother or father! Her silhouette disappeared over the horizon, their curses still echoing in the air.

Her steps led her to the edge of the valley. She had always heard that it was dark, full of horrific nightmares. She hesitated for a moment, thinking she had lost her way. It wasn't pitch darkness that faced her, but the colors of faint twilight. She heard sounds that resembled the dawn chorus of songbirds. She took a deep breath, held it in her chest as if preparing to dive into the ocean's depths, and continued moving forward. She walked with her eyes shut, feeling under her feet the softness of tender grass. A breeze blew through her hair, and from time to time gentle touches caressed her cheeks; she guessed them to be the wings of small birds and butterflies. She opened her eyes when she felt the touch of the ground changing beneath her feet. Instead of grass, she sensed small pebbles sliding under her footsteps. She found herself at the foot of a tall mountain, the top of which her eyes didn't reach. She took another deep breath, after which she started climbing, with the aid of jutting stones she clung to with both hands, while searching for a safe stone on which to place her next step. She advanced slowly and steadily, chanting a silent incantation, careful not to look down. "Show me the naked Truth." She whispered it over and over. She opened her eyes, the words still echoing upon her lips, after feeling a warm embrace. She found herself facing a gate of golden sunbeams,

each ray ending in a small palm. The tender palms caressed her, leading her to the river that lay beyond them. She inhaled deeply once again, after which she stretched over the surface of the water and shut her eyes. This part of the journey seemed to take an extraordinarily long time, as though time itself had frozen, as if it were one long extended day with no night. The surface of the water rippled, carrying her on her way, lulling her into a deep sleep.

She didn't know how long she slept. She woke to find the sky painted with the colors of dusk. She sat up and found a dirt road stretching out before her eyes. Her steps led her to its end, until she faced a dusty mirror hanging from one corner, its other side swinging loose. She reached out to wipe its dusty face. The door opened wide as soon as her features were reflected in the mirror with the broken edge. She stepped into the dim interior, chanting her incantation: "Show me the naked Truth." She heard the words that everyone in the cursed city had always repeated, as being the cause of the cursed misery that had befallen them: "Objects in the mirror are closer than they appear."

She sat cross-legged in front of the outstretched palms. She raised her head to face the surface of the mirror, which had splintered and shattered until it resembled the mosaic that made up her own features. A sudden dazzling light illuminated the earth. The lead lining of the seer's mirror shattered, and the lead safe of her heart cracked. Sweet notes arose from the graceful fingers. They began with a sad solo violin, rising to the pinnacle of melancholy. The notes followed, wave after wave, overlapping and complementing one another. They rose and fell in succession, like waves pulling the soul in their ebb toward the depths of pain, and returning it to the shore once again, with a flow that was saturated with glimpses of hope. The girl's eyes filled with tears. She felt small colorful flowers blooming in the cracks of her assembled features, watered by her flowing tears. The tones faded, and the seer's fingers embraced her small palms as rain poured heavily outside, cleansing the world.

Poetry

Heads — Tails

By **Reem Abbas**

This time going home I deracinated much of my intimaa', leaving the riot of my languages exposed on ajnabi soil. Where my grandmother spoke in her mother language I heard a mirror language speak back, fissuring a world of care into wound. Where are the nas bila qiyaas of that eden you storied to me. You once fed the lion head of this family but it has since declared itself nawawi. The milk extracted from your breasts mixes with dam. In a salt eyed conversation you confess a shoq for the abuser & recite shi'r he wrote you. I write lines like him, laki. Maqsad qasidati is rebellion. Tracing blood lines through maps fosters healing by lies. Sekkeh is Farsi for coin & transports me to Damascene sikkehs of memory: winding paths that wrap around tilting houses with marble courtyards & narrow doors. These languages spill gas & oil; their lines a fated game of shir /khaat. Chinks & shards: healing the colonial wound is a museum of mirrors. What, asks the orphan girl of my mother's past, will become of her story. Gunpowder khols her eyes & makes the blue pop, draws more sympathy from onlooking ajaaneb. My iraada for intimaa' is a weed that wont give. Its will to live strong as seductive as quwwa. The breast that fed the beast had no power, sheds milk tears. Rab al usra: godhead of the family. The patriarch, like me, pled refracted tongues.

Poetry

The Girl by the Window (1893) by Edvard Munch. Original from The Art Institute of Chicago. © Rawpixel

The Only Stranger Here

By **Duna Ghali**

For Karen Blixen;
Baroness Karen Blixen (1885-1962) was a Danish author who wrote in English and Danish. Her most well-known work is *Out of Africa* (1937).

Translated by
Layla AlAmmar

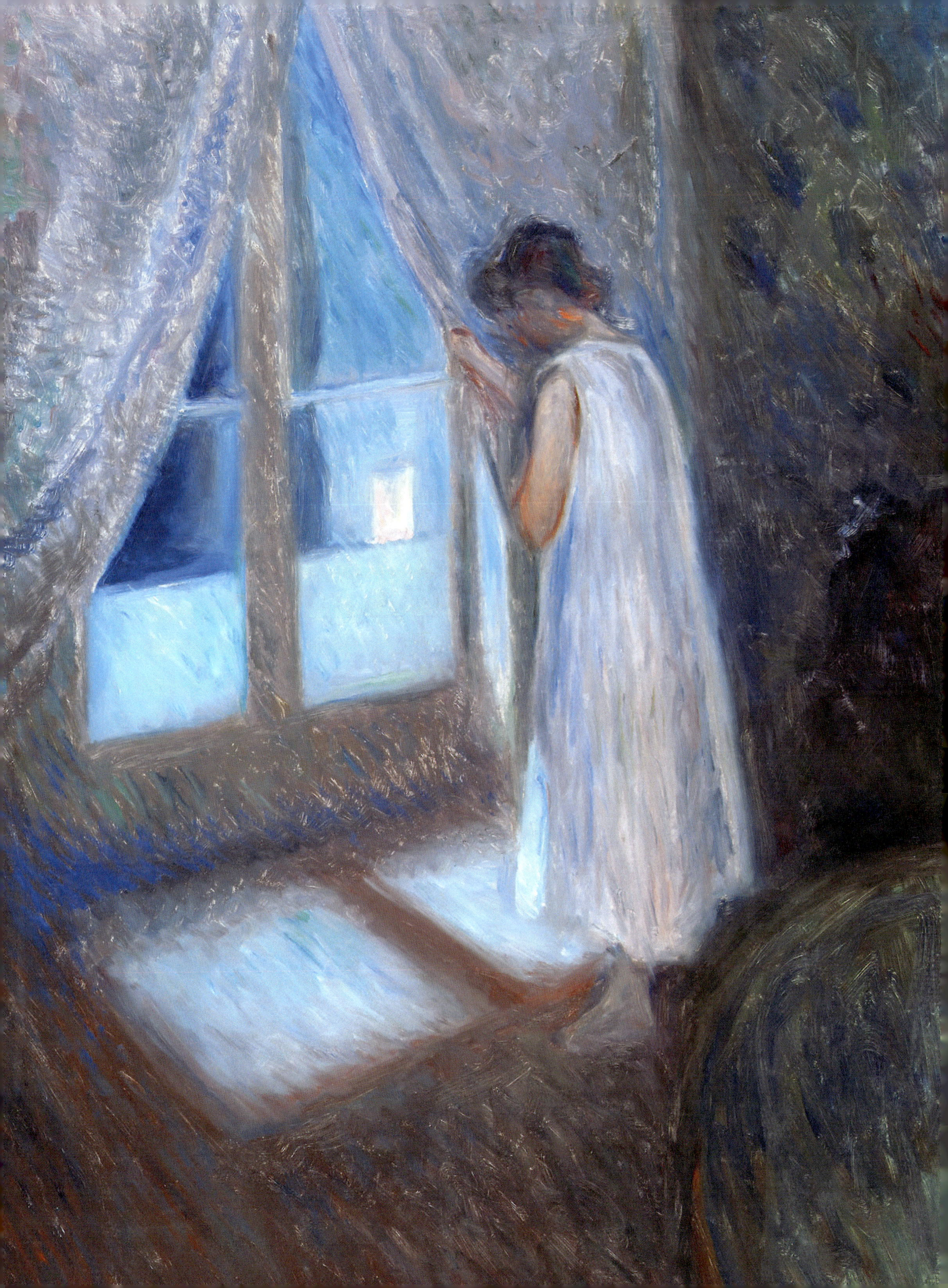

The scar stalks her like a curse. Perhaps not the scar exactly. It may be the shadow of an unwritten history. A coffee-colored nostalgia. A crescent bloating that refuses to settle into form. The sign of distinct exile. It hides. It protrudes. Repressed, monstrous cravings. Or is it a fertilized egg refusing to give up?

When she wakes, the image that greets her is foggy and unbound. There's no trace of even a small joy in the light seeping through the curtains. In that rectangular mirror are only the cloudy remnants of nights gone by, bolstered by columns of pain. No, it wasn't a nightmare. She rises and approaches the second mirror, the one on the dressing table. She takes her time. Illusion is her god. Or perhaps the moist breath permeating the room has fused with kohl and penetrated the layers of silver paint to convince the mirror to reflect this face.

She rushes to the bathroom and empties her bladder. She walks with this face of hers that she knows. Always a confrontation with her reflection. There's no escaping the ferocious assault.

Once, shards of a mirror were found. The archeologists said the mirror had belonged to Cleopatra. Shiny and pure shards, from a mirror that had, no doubt, broken on its own. No one knew if this was before or after she ingested the poison that killed her. It was the glimpse of a final siege that shattered her mirror. No one dared gather its pieces.

The bathroom light is artificial and white, sucking the blood from her cheeks and magnifying a yellow face questioning its puffiness. The architects who built this house had told her that one of the most difficult tasks would be choosing the right bathroom lighting! She pushes her face deep into a black towel and tries to erase her memory. Rubbing her face in the damp embrace of the fabric, trying to awaken the face of her youth. She scoffs. A strangled sound. With patience and sympathy, the weave of the towel soaks up each fiery exhalation.

In her remote home, north of Copenhagen, she goes exploring the hall of mirrors. Was this woman the enemy, or had the devil painted his face so that the morning would not be just another morning? In the distance, a radio blares. Boring local news. She prefers global stations that bring light and fluffy dispatches, easy to digest, nothing that would ruin the morning. A morning just like all other mornings around the world. Mornings that contain all that's left of the world's innocence. She would never dare say she wants for anything. Oh, if she could inspect the backs of the mirrors the way children do! At a turn in the corridor, overlooking the salon, she lowers her hand to reveal her face. The mirror hanging on the wall is neutral. It won't hide the truth. In this spot, the light gives up its conquest. The gleaming mahogany stirs no emotion, nor does it allow the present to be refreshed. She doesn't remember closing those heavy velvet drapes. Perhaps a splash of oil rests on the pupil of her eye.

In the salon, she hears a voice chasing the girl. A boy from her youth. Or perhaps a lover just back from a long journey. A known elegance and a habitual carelessness. She makes her way to the window, casually greeting the face that peers out of the Biedermeier frame. A flirtation that registers no swelling. She pauses and lets out a laugh, chasing the years away from her face. A special offer for a lazy Monday!

She is a creature expelled from its world. This entire house is in perfect harmony with itself, self-contained, just a hint of reality, and yet utterly without care for its surroundings. She is the only stranger here, and in each room there is a shining mirror.* No matter the frame, no matter the era. With them, the day is busy, armed with imagination and with pens the color of astonishment and anxiety.

Champagne in hand and fur around her shoulders, the day's agenda stretches before her. She greets the guests with a sarcastic smile, one after the next, drifting from room to room. Every once in a while, a mirror will take her aside or another will whistle to her from a distance or call her over with a wink.

Is there anything more orientalist and captivating than this! To treat our scars by acquiring mirrors that reveal and uncover. 'Listen here, clever one,' says she who is not without her own conservative brand of romance. 'Oh, lady of the distant desert, the thirst in that reflection is no mirage. It's over! The soul has been struck and rivers of champagne will not heal it.

---

* *There is an old folkloric saying that refers to the stranger's mirror as "always shining," where the stranger is the woman who leaves her parents' home to marry and live with her husband's family.*

Agitated Air:
Poems After Ibn Arabi

Yasmine Seale & Robin Moger

Born in Murcia in 1165, Ibn Arabi was a prolific Muslim philosopher and poet. He travelled extensively before settling in Damascus, where he died in 1240. *Tarjuman al-Ashwaq*, or *The Interpreter of Desires*, is a cycle of sixty-one Arabic poems. They speak of loss and bewilderment, a spiritual and sensual yearning for the divine, and a hunger for communion in which near and far collapse.

Agitated Air—the third title from Tenement Press—is a correspondence in poems between Istanbul and Cape Town, following the wake of *The Interpreter of Desires*. Collaborating at a distance, Yasmine Seale and Robin Moger work in close counterpoint, making separate translations of each poem, exchanging them, then writing new poems in response to what they receive. The process continues until they are exhausted, and then a new chain begins.

Translated and retranslated, these poems fray and eddy and, their themes of intimacy ac-ross distance made various, sing back and forth, circling and never landing. Absence and approach, knowing and unknowing, failure and repetition: Ibn Arabi's cycle of ecstatic love shimmers with turbulence. Seale and Moger move into and against these contending drifts, finding in the play of dissatisfaction and endurance a prompt for new poetry.

Antiphonal, intimate and virtuoso, these variations respond to the sense that the interpretation of desires can be endless—it can dance this way and that, and then turn and turn again. The exchange of voices, singing lines that meet and part, pick up on the presence of the lover and the beloved in the poems; as Yasmine Seale and Robin Moger pass each newly wrought phrase back and forth between them, the distance between Seale in Istanbul and Moger in Cape Town is bridged, and so are the centuries that separate us from Ibn Arabi, his motifs, his mystical ascents and descents, and his anguished yearning. This is translation as intrepid and inspired re-visioning, a form of poetry of its own, as forged by Edward FitzGerald, Ezra Pound and Anne Carson.
—Marina Warner

Agitated Air creates wonderful and vulnerable ways into knowing as yearning: source texts and original responses, expansions and contractions, song and sigh.
—Vahni Capildeo

Distance, and desire ruins me. To meet is no relief. Come or go, desire hardly cares.

I can be away and floored by longing, but it doesn't help when we're together. Longing: without and in her company.

Tenement Press 3, MMXXII
ISBN 978-1-8380200-4-0

www.tenementpress.com

Poetry

Ash-sha'b Yurid Isqat an-Nizam

By **Hilal Badr**

Translated by Ghada Alatrash

A shout awakens me; someone is yelling, "*Ash-sha'b yurid isqat an-nizam* [The People want to bring down the regime]." Does anyone believe this? I don't.

I think that the voice came through the window. No, not through the window. My wife is flipping through TV channels, one after another. For some reason, she stops for a moment, and then continues. Surely the shouts must've come through one of the channels.

I look at the bird that I'd bought a short while ago and listen as it chirps, hoping that it might console me in my distress. It is at this moment that a silly analogy comes to mind—that in the best states of my being, I resemble this bird; and that my country, in all of its states, resembles this cage. The bird suddenly interrupts my contemplation and shouts, "*Ash-sha'b yurid isqat an-nizam*. [The People want to bring down the regime]." I stand in disbelief.

Ahmed Akacha © Pexels

Hoping that she will validate my insanity, I ask my wife if she heard the bird shouting "*Ash-sha'b yurid isqat an-nizam* [The People want to bring down the regime]." She does not reply with a yes or a no, but with, "And what do you expect a bird in a cage to shout?"

I bend over the sink in the bathroom where the crazy washing machine is spinning. I have not washed my face for a week. I hear a rattling noise, *Ash-sha'b yurid isqat an-nizam* [The People want to bring down the regime]. I wonder if the words are pouring out of the faucet of the sink or from the drainage hole. There is no other mouth in this bathroom! Or perhaps they are coming from the washing machine that continues to spin, shouting out its angry cries, while pretending that she has nothing to do with what's happening. But who does he think she's fooling!

I hear this cry like a song echoing in my ear. I hear it like a chant made with the chaotic noises of the day, the horns of cars, the voices of merchants strolling through the streets, and I hear it in the panting of the people. I hear it like a song sung to the beats of their anxious footsteps: *Ash-sha'b yurid isqat an-nizam* [The People want to bring down the regime]."

I don't want anything, I don't need anything, I have fulfilled all my life's ambitions. I fell in love, got married, had children, held a secure job for 30 years, and I sketched and wrote down every thought that has crossed my mind, most of which were trivial, although a few proved to be great. I have produced enough books, and I have taken time to rest. What more can I want? I want nothing but what the people want, and I have heard the people with my two ears, shouting at the top of their lungs, "*Ash-sha'b yurid isqat an-nizam* [The People want to bring down the regime]."

As for me—a poet who has nothing to do with politics, has never belonged to a political party in his life, and is neither pro or anti-regime—I confess to you that I may not fully grasp the meaning of this cry and whether it came at the right time or if it were a product of mere excitement. But what I do know is that it came following all the other cries, "We love you, Syria," "Freedom, Freedom, Freedom," "The Syrian people will not be humiliated," and "There is no fear after today." One cry that harvested them all; one cry that bundled them all together as one and clenched its fist tight around them; one cry, the mother of all cries, shouted by the people. An outcry, as in the words of those who like poetic metaphors, that darted from the furnace of their hearts, passing through the lining of their larynxes, solidified and hardened by their clenching teeth, anointed with the saliva and oil of their tongues, and shot like a bullet from the nozzle of their mouths. And here I am, standing at my windowsill, hidden in complete darkness, and I can hear an outcry from a man I do not recognize. I stare at his reflection in the glass, but I don't see him, for he is still hiding inside of me; "*Ash-sha'b yurid isqat an-nizam* [The People want to bring down the regime]."

Editor's note: Hilal Badr is the pen name of a Syrian poet.

Poetry

The Patient Mirror

By Qassim Majeed

Translated by Zeena Faulk

I'm uncertain . . .
whether the ceiling fan that booms like a war tank
will continue its rotation to the end of summer.

*

And this night, with its long teeth,
morphs into an enormous storm cloud
that hovers above the wilderness of memory
after we opened the door to oblivion,
to store five photographs of the deceased
and a sixth photo of me.
I wait. I prop my face up with a palm.

Igra © Pexels

The sun coughs sickly in the yard.
And we inhale the scent of the air
after the downpour washes it up.
But only she—the mirror—
endures the dust and drizzle alike.

*

As soon as dawn breaks,
we awaken to the roar of the masjid's thirty loudspeakers.
My grandson lifts his head in a jolt
"Where's that sound coming from?"

*

My granddaughter, Teeba,
doodles on the gate in white chalk.
She writes some times-tables
and draws half a map of Iraq.

*

Each dwelling leans on the next,
and the roads . . .
they suffer from a permanent ailment.

*

At midday, the teaboy
shutters his teashop.
The fortune-teller opens
his henna-streaked door.

*

Days roll toward the unknown,
without justifying blunders
or offering answers
to questions that give sorrow.
What shouldn't be forgiven is that
you're alive in a time
that has no fixed face—not even in the mirror.

ARABLIT STORY PRIZE

This is the fourth year of the ArabLit Story Prize, which invites submissions of contemporary and classic Arabic short stories, paired with English translations. Judges select those stories that stand out for their freshness, wit, and depth of emotion, while also looking at how the Arabic original and English translation mirror one another.

Each year, three judges read through submissions, blindly, in both Arabic and English. This year, five stories were shortlisted by judges Layla AlAmmar, Leri Price, and Nadia Ghanem:

Rasha Abbas's "You Can Call Me Velvet"
(تستطيع أن تدعوني مخمل), as translated by Katharine Halls

Karima Ahdad's "The Baffling Case of the Man Called Ahmet Yilmaz"
(الحالة المحيّرة للمدعوّ أحمت يلماز), as translated by Katherine Van de Vate

Mustafa Taj Aldeen Almosa's "How Kind They Are"
(كم هم لطفاء), as translated by Maisaa Tanjour & Alice Holttum

Ahmed Magdy Hammam's "The Hemingway Man"
(خدعة هيمنجواي), as translated by Burnaby Hawkes

Said Takieddine's "Camphor Forestland"
(غابة الكافور), as translated by Dima El-Mouallem

Mustafa Taj Aldeen Almosa's "How Kind They Are,"
co-translated by Maisaa Tanjour and Alice Holttum,
was chosen as the 2021 winner.

How Kind They Are

By **Mustafa Taj Aldeen Almosa**, translated by **Maisaa Tanjour & Alice Holttum**

For ten years, my hair has caused me untold suffering. I always let it grow long, only trimming it very occasionally. It is frizzy but I really wish it was silky soft. Over these years I have tried many creams and oils, but it has remained frizzy. When I walk down the street, the lightest gust of wind is enough to make me look like a ghoul. Kids run from me as if I am the snake-haired Medusa herself. Oh, how my long hair has exasperated me and not been what I wanted.

They arrested me yesterday evening. The patrol head greeted me in his own way, and I was very surprised: instead of shaking my hand, he warmly shook my face with his fist, causing one of my teeth to fly from my mouth and land on the street. I read once that certain nations have peculiar habits when it comes to handshakes—kissing noses, for example. I secretly wondered if the patrol head was one of those people. After that, he lovingly kicked me into a car and we went to the security department.

Artwork by Zahra Marwan

* *Ali Aqla Arsan is a Syrian politician, writer and president of the Arab Writers Union from 1969 to 2005. His policies conformed to those of the Syrian ruling party and attempted to oppress and silence the voices of free Syrian writers.*

** *Michel Kilo is a Syrian dissident writer and human rights activist.*

I was very upset about my knocked-out tooth; I imagined one of the local kids treading on it, crushing it during a game of football.

At the security department, they affectionately hurled me into a cramped cell. There were dozens of young men in there and I could only just squeeze into the corner. Terrifying shrieks were penetrating our cell from all directions. How lucky those neighbors were: they had televisions to watch the Barcelona vs Real Madrid match and were raucously cheering the teams on.

An hour passed as I looked through a skylight in the roof of the cell, watching the night creeping up and the moon scattering feeble light over our bodies. By chance I noticed something written on the wall to my right: *I love you, Lina*. The word 'love' made me sigh. I opened my mouth and grabbed another tooth that was on the verge of falling out. I used it to scratch the following sentence under the first one: *This man loves you, Lina. Damn you! You must understand this fact. Damn you, too, Samira, because I love you, but you act like this man's Lina.* Then I drew a heart pierced by a sharp arrow. When I had finished, I put my tooth in my shirt pocket. Oh, what can I say about young women! They never believe that men have equal rights nowadays!

I almost suffocated in the silence of those young men. I turned to my right and gasped when I saw my neighbor.

"Ali Aqla Arsan! *" I exclaimed. You're here too? Hello, it's nice to meet you."

"Hi! But I'm not Ali Aqla Arsan."

Naturally, this was a little trick of my own invention; I often used it on the south route bus to start a conversation with whomever was sitting next to me.

At that moment, the door of the cell opened and the jailer cried out my name. I stood up happily, muttering, "Finally, time for dinner!"

I walked to the door and, before exiting, asked the others, "Want anything from outside?"

Frankly, I was afraid that someone might ask for a kilo of oranges, or a kilo of apples … or a Kilo of Michel**—the market had actually closed hours ago. No one uttered a word, so I sighed in relief and went away. The jailer kicked my legs and I fell. He grabbed my right leg, his colleague my left, and they dragged me quickly along a long gloomy corridor. How considerate of them: they did not want me to walk and were protecting my legs from exhaustion. Truly, I felt embarrassed by their kindness.

In the Inspector's room, there was a thin, naked young man on the floor. He was unconscious and covered in blood. The Inspector was taking photos of him on his mobile phone. When he had finished, one of the jailers took the young man out. The Inspector looked at me. I smiled at him. "Why is your hair so long, you asshole?" he shouted at me.

My God: asshole. What a beautiful, kind word, sounding like a sweet melody coming from a piano. It was my uncle's favorite word, what he always called me when we played cards with our friends.

"It's because the barber in our neighborhood is a dissident, so I boycotted him as soon as the cosmic conspiracy against our country started."

"A dissident? Give me his name and address!"

"His name is Taj Aldeen. He lives in the fourth grave to the right of the olive tree, in the southern graveyard."

The Inspector gave the address to the jailers and

THE WINNER

ARABLIT STORY PRIZE

2021

*** *A Syrian pro-regime television channel known for disseminating government propaganda and sanctioned by the EU in 2011 for inciting violence.*

ordered them to fetch the so-called Taj immediately. I was over the moon: only the security services would have the ability to reach into the afterworld to bring me back my father, who had passed away a year ago, I thought.

The Inspector smiled maliciously as he tied my hands behind my back. Then he gathered my long hair in his hand and tied to it a thick rope. He passed this rope through a metal ring that was hanging from the ceiling. He pulled the rope, assisted by the jailer, and my body rose up. I was dangling from the ceiling by my hair. Wow! I was mesmerized by this amusing notion. I was like a swing. The Inspector started pushing my body towards the jailer and the jailer pushed it back. They were laughing like two little children. I laughed with them; I really liked this game and I sang them a Fairouz song, *Yara*. But after a few minutes the Inspector yawned and left the room with the jailer to go to sleep for a while, leaving me there alone, hanging from the ceiling by my hair. I was very sad. Why had they not stayed to play with me? What did they have to lose? We had all been enjoying this funny game, the three of us. How kind the Inspector was. But unfortunately, he had forgotten to take my photo with his mobile phone, so I had lost a unique opportunity for fame. I would have had fans, and girls would have chased me wherever I went.

After a few hours, blood started to trickle from my forehead over my face. Soon some flies flew up to drink ravenously. After they had finished, one of them came and landed on my nose, smiled at me and said, "Thank you. Your blood is a true delicacy."

"You're welcome, my friend. I'm happily at your service."

"Can I ask you something?"

"Please do."

"Do you believe in God?"

"Um … To be honest, hanging like this, I can't possibly believe in anything."

"You mean you're an atheist."

"I remember being a believer last Tuesday."

We both remained silent for a moment, then I exhaled deeply and said, "To be honest, my friend, I don't believe in unreciprocated faith. I believe in faith and counter-faith, and since I was a child I've felt that God doesn't believe in me."

"Hmm."

Suddenly the Inspector entered the room; the flies panicked and flew off my face. "Goodbye, my love," whispered the one that had spoken to me as it flew away.

The Inspector ordered the jailer to get me down and take me back to the cell. I wanted to ask about dinner, but the jailer kicked my legs again and I fell. He grabbed me by the legs and dragged me back along the gloomy corridor.

From the door of one of the cells along the corridor came the sound of someone screaming. His voice was very similar to my father's. Delighted, I screamed back, "How are you, Dad? Don't worry about me—the people here are very kind, rest assured. Later, they're going to send us to Addounia TV***, where I'll talk on camera about our important literary experiences. Then we'll take a souvenir photo with the host in the 'Misleading News' section. After that, we'll go home and drink our best *araq*. Don't worry, Dad. Do you have any cigarettes? Just a couple of cigarettes, please, for the sake of the Soviet Union! Please—I'm dying for a cigarette."

Apparently, my father couldn't hear me over the screams of the Barcelona and Real Madrid supporters.

The jailer opened the door to my cell while I lay on the floor. "My father being brought back from the afterworld by the security services will put the *fuqaha* in a very embarrassing position before believers," I thought. "I hope that God will inspire them with the right interpretation."

Then my sweet romantic jailer lifted me up in his arms as if I was his beloved, and threw me gently into the cell.

Under the faint light of the moon penetrating the room through the skylight, I tried to look for Ali Aqla Arsan, but one of the men tapped me on the shoulder and whispered, "Do you know anything about corpses?"

"Yes, I do—most of my family died in my arms."

"Please, can you check if this guy's dead or not? I can't see well enough."

I looked where he was pointing and saw the thin naked man from before. I leant over him and took his head in between my hands, lifting it towards the moonlight. I moved my face toward his until our noses touched. I stared deeply into his eyes and saw my face clearly reflected in them … I gasped sharply. My frizzy hair was silky soft; I couldn't believe it. I let the young man's head fall to the floor and caressed my hair. Only then was I certain that it really had become as soft as silk.

My mind soared with happiness. I stood in the middle of the cell laughing madly. I clapped my hands and swayed joyfully. Everyone applauded me, including Lina and Samira from the wall. They cheered my primitive dance. I danced for a long time beside the corpse of the thin young man. I danced ecstatically like a drunk jester and, through the small skylight in the roof, the moon wept some more light upon us from above.

You Can Call Me Velvet

By **Rasha Abbas**, translated by **Katharine Halls**

What breaks us saves us. Amen. My name isn't important. I'm 24 years old. You can call me Velvet.

You're thinking as you look at me that you couldn't stand it if I were your daughter, or friends with your daughter. Nobody can blame you for that. There are the tattoos, for a start. The tattoos that cover my whole arm, some of which have been defaced by time—or by me, intentionally, especially the names of men I have loved. Some of them are written in languages I don't know. Never once have I failed to identify a look of contempt when it is aimed in my direction. Of course you wouldn't want a daughter like me; I'm not even the type of girl you might want for yourself, a little indiscretion to keep the mid-life blues at bay. I can see that, and I'm not offended.

My name isn't important. I'm 20 years old. First I went to university to study translation.
I got bored of it within a month. I thought about changing subjects, but it was too late by then, so I decided to quit university and become an actor. Although it seemed easy to begin with, I never got anywhere with it. The same thing had happened before, when I thought I had a gift for drawing then failed the art school entrance exam. My dad was cleaning the floor when I arrived home with a new tattoo—a tiger—to celebrate my decision to drop out. Dad listened to me as he studied the raised, inflamed bumps of the tattoo. He said I'd started behaving like my mother, which filled him with fear. I told him that acting was a very well paid line of work, and that I'd make sure he was well taken care of. I regretted it later. Sure, he didn't comment when I started staying away from the house for days at a time, and I was able to use auditions and meetings with directors as excuses for trips to the city, but every time he found something of mine dumped on the floor as he was cleaning, he'd start yelling, begging me to leave him to live by himself and saying that he wanted to get married again. But then he'd calm down and ask when I was going to start bringing in some wages. I began to wish he'd get back together with his second wife and forget about us again, like he did after my mum left. He tried very hard at the time to find out whether her leaving had anything to do with us. The few occasions he showed any interest in my life—brief moments when his attention wasn't occupied by his new wife—were when he went into my bedroom in my absence to go through my mobile phone and check if I was in contact with my mother. Still, I wish things could go back to how they were then, instead of him sitting here all day long watching me like a hawk.

My name isn't important. I'm 27 years old. I'd appreciate it if you could give me a cigarette.
Do you know why I seem like this? The difference between us is that you possess roots struck deep in the earth. That is why you look clean and why your smile is so nice, while I seem untrustworthy. What breaks us saves us. It's practically a law. When I used to get told off as a teenager it was said to me that I was a plant of the Devil, with no roots. It didn't hurt: it was a remark made in anger and in haste, but in truth it was highly perceptive. Or perhaps I simply adopted it. I would observe what was around me to find out why I was like this, so removed from familiarities and deep entanglements, from the intimacy that I saw coursing vigorously through everything around me and yet avoiding me. I could see their roots clearly, struck in the mirror at home where a young woman would stand surveying her appearance before she went out, and where relatives and siblings and friends appeared in every corner knowing exactly what was to be done and what was to be said such that they seem trained for it, amazingly, trained for the intercourse of daily life, for conflict, for purchasing the right things: that intimacy flowed easily through all those interlocking channels, and I didn't always feel welcome, though I remember I did try many times to copy what I saw, and I wasn't bad at it but that earth just wasn't my

earth: I could see clearly how it had spat me out, how I didn't sprout and flourish like my antagonists, them, the ones with roots, who managed to smash-and-grab everything I had ever wanted. It took time for me to find out, not long ago at all, that what breaks us saves us, and that my medals had been in my pocket all along, and when I came to see them, poking solidly out of the dust and dirt, cheap elements, when the Earth moved and flipped itself inside out, the glory went to the artful plant that was scattered and strewn so lightly on the breeze, all of it. So let the Lord's name be praised, and let his word come down on the earth below like the blow of a sword—the glory went to me and to my flighty blue element, to the ugly third eye that had opened up in my chest which for so long I was not allowed to refer to other than as a scar. The end times had come and the earth was mine! I arrived in this city a year ago. I thought I'd feel familiarity at last among all the other freaks that inhabit this place. I thought I wouldn't be a stranger here like I was back home. But it didn't happen. Do you know how impossible it is to find a job? They might think I look kooky, cute—the blue hair, the facial piercings, the tattoos—but nobody will trust me with a job. Of course, on the day of the interview I can wear clean clothes and take out the piercings and hide my arms under long sleeves, but that's not the point: these appearances exist to help us identify each other, so we don't have to bother dealing with those who are a burden to us. We are rootless, that is the story. Not for one day was it easy, and that's why I'm here. I feel truly cold from standing in the street talking to people who are in such a rush.

My name isn't important. I'm 17 years old. You can call me Velvet.
I was home alone. I phoned my father to ask for money to buy food. He asked me to come by without saying anything to his wife, so I hung up and went out to the park. I sat for a while, and some boys who were sitting there tried to say hi to me by sending a beggar boy to give me some chewing gum. I quickly got up and hurried to another corner of the park, where there was a children's playground. I chose an empty wooden bench to sit on. A few minutes later a woman sat down next to me. She was slim and tall and dark-skinned and wore a headscarf, and looked like she was in her forties. She seemed to have very deep roots, and no need for anybody else's opinion of her life. Out of a clean bag she took a falafel sandwich, and broke off half of it for me. I was mortified, because my tears began to spill out of their own accord, heavily, as soon as I put it in my mouth. The bread was warm and the falafel was still hot. The woman had roots indeed, just as I'd imagined, because she didn't inundate me with pity. She waited till I'd calmed down a bit before telling me, without asking me anything, that she worked for a literacy programme in the countryside, that I should get a job so I wouldn't feel so bad, and that I could work for them. She asked about my family and I said they were away. She looked like she disapproved of that and asked for our home phone number. I was drawn, somehow, strangely, into giving it to her, without changing a number like I could easily have done. I thanked her and went home, feeling regretful, because I'd meet a grim fate if my family found out that I'd been airing our problems to an unknown woman in a park. I hoped she wouldn't call, but she did.

My name isn't important. I'm 26 years old. You can call me Velvet.
Don't touch me unless you want to get kicked out of the bar. The enormous bouncer is awaiting his evening's entertainment: customers who lose control, whom he likes to drag out of the bar in a humiliating fashion. You can look at me or my female colleagues as much as you like here. I've been told I should smile at you and put up with your sexual innuendoes while I'm taking your order, but you can't touch me or the enormous bouncer will throw you out. I carry a small knife in the folds of

my dress, and one day I think I won't hesitate to use it. I haven't yet. Here they call me Velvet, and you can call me that too.

My name isn't important. I'm 30 years old. You can call me Velvet, and give me a cigarette.
I really like smoking, but I can't always afford to buy cigarettes. When I roll, the contents fall out before I can smoke them, and the paper burns up pretty quickly by itself. Don't worry, I have a place to sleep, with relatives of mine who live in this city. But I feel awkward, because it isn't my home, and I don't pay the rent, so it's better if they don't see me in the daytime and I get back after they've gone to bed. It's eleven now, not long until I can head home. I don't do sex work, contrary to what you think, I just like these clothes; I like these artificial little cheerful things and their synthetic, trashy feel. Although I feel flattered by your question—do I provide sexual services?—and respect your loneliness, unfortunately all I can do is tell you my story so you will feel like you've had a special experience. In exchange all I ask is that you give me a cigarette to smoke while I'm waiting for the bus to come so I can go home and sleep tonight.

My name isn't important. I'm 17 years old. You can call me Velvet.
The phone rang for a long time. I was scared to pick up; I wanted the woman from the park, who I suspected was the one calling, to simply think that the house was empty and that no-one would ever reply. Maybe then she'd stop calling, and my mum, if she ever came home, wouldn't find out I'd been talking to strangers about our home life and our problems. Then I decided I would answer, and mask my voice, and lie to her that she'd got the wrong number. It was her, as I'd expected. She asked after me. Instead of continuing with my plan, I pretended I was a sister. She said: Is she often out of the house? I didn't say anything, then she addressed me by my name; my name isn't important. I put the phone down and left the house.

My name isn't important. I'm 26 years old. You can call me Velvet.
The enormous bouncer isn't the person I go out with, but don't try to touch me while I'm working, otherwise he will kick you out. In the end it was me that got kicked out. All of that for her; her name isn't important either. I became convinced that she was the one for me. She was a single clear point amid all the bad that was taking place. She had a lovely-looking pointed nose. She was struggling to handle the punter that kept calling her over on the pretext of ordering something so he could talk to her and embarrass her. Her pale face was red and I could see how he was making her flinch. I went over to the table without hesitation, touching the small knife in the pocket of my dress. Did the customer touch you, Velvet? She was flustered as she answered the question, and it was because of that that the manager of the bar asked me to leave. I never saw the woman for whose sake I was kicked out again. I talked to her once, many years later, and learned that she had gone back to her family home and then got married, and that now she has many beautiful children to fill her house. She has struck root in blessed earth while I am still riding the winds, suspended in this terrestrial dome by my defaced tattoos and my blue hair.

My name isn't important. I'm 30 years old. You can call me Velvet.
I spent longer than I should have trying to talk to someone outside, and the last train departed. It wouldn't be the first time I'd spent the night in the street. I battled my way through the torrents of rain, the heaviest downpour I had seen in years; the cheap hair dye I used wasn't going to hold out for long. I'm thirty years old and my name isn't important. In a world of ice I would have been called a prophetess: I carry loneliness on my shoulders so that others in these drugged torpid cities do not have to and my story drips droplets of blue hair dye all along the road. Upon these traces my legend, finally, will flourish and sprout from the heart of the earth into

wooden benches for the lost and forlorn whose color, blue, will not run in the rain, and people will sit there waiting for you, people who take things to eat out of clean bags they packed at home and there they will ask you, press you, for your home phone number.

The Baffling Case of the Man Called Ahmet Yilmaz

By **Karima Ahdad**, translated by **Katherine Van de Vate**

His bald spot gleaming in the overhead light, the airport border official raised his head and scrutinized the traveler in front of him. With a sneer, he handed him back his dark red passport.

"Welcome, Ahmet Yilmaz Bey!"

Ahmet felt his face flush. He picked up his passport and stalked off through the crowds in Atatürk Airport, jerking his suitcase violently behind him. It was the first time he'd been embarrassed by his Turkish name, the one he'd chosen when he turned 30, after living in Turkey for six years.

"Ahmet Yilmaz!" How often had he swelled with pride when he said those words. When people asked him his name, he replied "Ahmet Yilmaz!" in a loud voice, articulating it slowly and clearly, almost boastfully. Everyone should hear it and know he was now Turkish in his own right.

Why does a person want to become something other than what he really is, he asked himself, as he contemplated his reflection in the glass doors of the airport. Today, for the first time, he felt like there was a pressure cooker instead of a brain inside his skull. What about his curly hair, his dark complexion, and his North African features? He hadn't given them a second thought in his rush to acquire Turkish citizenship and change his name from Ahmad al-Mansuri to Ahmet Yilmaz.

He got into a taxi and headed towards his home in Üsküdar, musing that some things in life can't be changed, like the past, or one's memories. A person can change the way he thinks, his car, or where he lives. He can alter his nose, his hair color, even his name. A person can change anything and everything about himself except his past. And for him, Ahmad al-Mansuri, it was that he'd been born in Morocco, not Turkey.

"What country are you from?" asked the taxi driver with a smile, squinting at him in the rear-view mirror.

Ahmad gazed through the window at the road and pretended he hadn't heard. Why did people continue to look down on him? Why did they still treat him like a foreigner? Why did they call him "yabancı"—foreigner—every time he took a taxi to the immigration office or even just to the supermarket? Why did his landlord treat him like he was an outsider who knew nothing about Turkey, and always tried to cheat him?

His Turkish was excellent; he spoke the language fluently. He was certainly not the first person to get Turkish citizenship and change his name. His Palestinian friend Mustafa Abu Khadra had changed his name to Mustafa Özdemir. His colleague, the Syrian refugee Muhammad al-Khabbaz, had become Mehmet Demir. And ever since Ahmad's wife had come from Morocco to join him four years ago, she too had longed for the day when she could take a Turkish name. He knew many people who hoped to become Turkish. Anyway, what was wrong with changing your name to a Turkish one?

"Names are only names; most of the time they don't mean anything," he consoled himself as he stared through the taxi window at the road, as dark and desolate as his mood. A thought suddenly hit him like a splash of cold water on his head: "So if that's the case, why do we try to change our names?"

When Ahmad first came to Turkey to study communications, the so-called "Turkish dream" had conquered the hearts of Moroccans, displacing their dreams of America and Europe. Romantic Turkish soap operas, long turquoise abayas and embroidered headscarves of every color, beautiful fair-skinned girls, their veils draped gracefully, the poetry of the great Mevlana Jalal al-Din Rumi and Shams Tabrizi, a huge array of Turkish food at cheap prices. Pictures of Ottoman palaces and mosques, the TV drama "Resurrection Ertuğrul," and the Facebook pages of President Erdoğan's many admirers. Ahmad was enchanted by it all, and captivated by the Turkish president's proud demeanor, his confident stride, and the fiery cadences of his speeches defending the world's Muslims.

He couldn't bear to wait any longer. Kissing his mother's lined palm and his fiancee Fatima's forehead, he promised his wife-to-be that he would soon bring her to join him in the most beautiful city in the world. A dusty brown suitcase in tow, he caught a plane to Istanbul, his heart full of anticipation and his mind filled with beguiling images. He used his university studies to establish himself in his new country, renting a room in a small apartment with a tall, blond, athletic Turk. He could not understand why this blue-eyed young man looked at him with disapproval whenever Ahmad talked about the glories of the Turkish nation and its president. When Ahmad came home from his university classes, he would find his housemate sprawled not on his own bed, but on Ahmad's, or wearing his clothes, or even using his bath towel and razor. Ahmad could not open his mouth or say a word of protest against the situation. Instead, he channeled his rage into his ambition to obtain Turkish citizenship.

And here he was, finally, Turkish.

But he derived no pleasure from gazing at the Bosphorus. He didn't enjoy eating milk pudding with pistachios or Adana kebab. He didn't appreciate Turkish music or believe that blue beads protected one from the evil eye. Whenever he watched the Turkish flag flutter in the breeze or sipped Turkish tea, he only felt an aching nostalgia for a glass of Moroccan tea suffused with fragrant mint leaves.

He suppressed that desire; maybe one day he would be able to see the world through Turkish eyes.

Exhausted from his convoluted thoughts, Ahmad reached home, where his wife Fatima had supper waiting. But before he could sit down, Fatima told him she'd just heard from the landlord that he wanted them to move out. Ahmad did not say a word. He looked at his plate of Iskender kebab with uncharacteristic distaste, then directed his glance towards a side table on which sat a heavy copper bust of Sultan Süleiman the Magnificent. He had bought it from a shop by the Galata Tower during his first year in Istanbul. How long ago the intoxicating joy of those days seemed! It was as if reality were determined to dash a man's hopes. Yet he had not given up on his dream for a moment, nor had he lost his respect for the president of this great nation.

Fatima turned on the television and began talking animatedly about the Hagia Sophia Museum, which had recently been converted back into a mosque. The sound of the television and Fatima's chatter jumbled together in Ahmad's head. Though he wasn't actually in a good mood, he laughed uproariously during supper as he entertained his wife with a joke about a goose that had unsuccessfully tried to fly. When the goose gave up and tried to walk again, she had forgotten how, and was obliged to spend the remainder of her days neither flying nor walking.

"Once you get your Turkish citizenship, what do you want to be called?" he asked Fatima, his tone now serious and his face downcast.

"Amina!" Fatima replied enthusiastically as she poured him a glass of Turkish tea.

"But that's an Arab name!" Ahmed said in astonishment.

"I know, but it's also the name of the Turkish President's wife," Fatima said with undiminished enthusiasm. She sat down across from him and gazed dreamily into the distance, her round face lit by the room's weak yellow light. "She's wonderful! I want to be like her one day."

Regarding her with an absent smile, Ahmad did not respond. He switched on his phone and scrolled through Facebook posts as he drank his tea. Lost in her reverie, Fatima sat motionless, absentmindedly holding her tulip-shaped glass.

Coming across a Facebook post that he liked, Ahmad read it out: "The first call to prayer in the Hagia Sophia after its conversion back into a mosque. We hope Sultan Erdoğan will now liberate the Aqsa Mosque in Jerusalem the same way he's given Hagia Sophia back to the Muslims."

Fatima said: "We need to find somewhere else to live. We only have a month."

Ahmad felt the blood rush to his head. Their landlord was an irascible, ultra-nationalist Turk. When they met to sign the rental contract, he looked Ahmad over from head to toe with a mistrustful gaze, as he chewed gum with a heavy smell of mint. He had grudgingly agreed to rent him the apartment on the grounds that Ahmet was an Arab. In actual fact, neither Ahmad nor his wife was Arab. They both came from a Moroccan city where almost everyone's first language was Amazigh. But there was no way to make this clueless Turk understand this. For him, there were only three kinds or classes of people in the world: Europeans, who had the highest status; Turks, who ranked slightly lower; and at the bottom, Arabs, the last people on earth to deserve respect or appreciation.

"So why do the Arabs flee their countries and infest the rest of the world, like fleas?" he once overheard a Turkish colleague ask. That colleague was like his landlord, not in how he looked, but in how he hated Arabs and felt superior to them.

But all of that had happened before Ahmad received his Turkish passport. Why would his landlord throw him out now, when he was a full citizen? He'd given up his real name, his identity, and his ties to his homeland so he could enjoy the same treatment as others in this country.

Now his landlord was saying he'd changed his mind and didn't want to rent to Arabs any more. His decision terrified Fatima—Ahmad could see the fear in her eyes—but she wasn't resentful. She was still attached to Turkey and to her dream of acquiring citizenship. Her only remaining link to Morocco was to its food, like couscous and lamb tajine with prunes.

Ahmad slammed his glass down and exclaimed: "I'm not leaving this place no matter what! He'll have to throw me out!"

Fatima stepped back fearfully. Leaning on the chair opposite him, she muttered:

"There are lots of houses nicer than this one in Üsküdar and other parts of Istanbul. We can find somewhere else." She fell silent for a moment, then said with a forced laugh: "Don't you remember the proverb: 'Moving house brings peace of mind?'"

All Fatima's efforts to calm her husband down ended in failure. The landlord came the following day to try and reach a solution. Fatima prepared tea and welcomed him like a king, an artificial smile fixed on her face as she set out the glasses on the sitting room table. When she was dealing with a Moroccan, she held her head high, but when she met a Turk, she would lower it deferentially. Even her back would suddenly develop an astonishing curve, as if it carried an invisible, heavy stone. Ahmad was mystified by his wife's astonishing ability to change her personality so quickly, and often asked himself if he behaved the same way in the presence of Turks.

He watched her angrily as she disappeared into the kitchen. But he was actually angry at himself and at the world. She was only a mirror reflecting him and all his shortcomings—his weakness, his servility, and his sense of alienation. She was the prism through which he viewed everything.

No longer able to suppress his fury, Ahmad turned toward the landlord. The pressure cooker inside his head had begun to whistle, and he felt as if he was about to lose his mind.

Placing a cigarette between his narrow blue lips, the landlord said arrogantly: "I've come to resolve this disagreement peacefully. I'll give you two months to find a new place."

His offer only enraged Ahmad further. He replied defiantly: "I'm not leaving this apartment until the end of the contract!"

Lighting his cigarette, the landlord replied nonchalantly: "I can't wait five more months. Two months is enough for you to find another place."

Ahmad hated smokers. He began coughing, not from the smoke but from the anger mounting inside him. "You have no reason to throw us out illegally!" he shouted.

The landlord interrupted him with a grimace: "There's a perfectly good reason, and I don't have to explain myself. I no longer want to rent my flat to Arabs."

Ahmad objected vociferously: "I am not an Arab! I'm a Turkish citizen now, the same as you!"

"Citizenship doesn't make you a Turk," said the landlord. "Only blood and birth can make you Turkish, nothing else."

Thrusting his agitated face into the landlord's, Ahmad declared: "I'm not leaving! Let's see what you can do about that!"

Unperturbed, the landlord replied: "You have no idea what I can do."

Fatima hurried back from the kitchen. In an effort to calm things down, she said with a smile: "Mr. Sirdar, I hope you'll go easy on us. My husband is rather short-tempered, as you see. He even acts like this with me. I hope you'll be good enough to extend our notice period. You know how hard it is to find an affordable apartment in Istanbul these days. We need more time to—"

"Get back in the kitchen!" Ahmad cut her off in Moroccan Arabic. "I'll sort things out with this prejudiced idiot!"

Sirdar stood up and stubbed out his cigarette in his tea glass. As he turned to leave, Fatima looked into her husband's eyes with irrational fear. Her hands shaking, she said in a quavering voice:

"Please forgive us, Mr. Sirdar! We promise we'll move out as quickly as possible."

The pressure cooker inside Ahmad's skull rose to a shriek. He was overcome by dizziness, unable to move or speak. Sirdar walked to the door without a backward glance. Collecting himself, Ahmad got to his feet. Flashing Fatima a look of furious contempt, he reached over to his right and grabbed the bust of Sultan Süleiman from the table. As the door closed behind Sirdar, Ahmad smashed the statue over his wife's head. With a wail, Fatima fell to the floor, awash in her own blood.

The Hemingway Man

By **Ahmed Magdy Hammam**, translated by **Burnaby Hawkes**

She loved music and books. Every day on her way to work and back, she used her earphones to listen to music and held a paperback in her hand. On this particular day, she was hurrying back from work when, at the corner of the street where she lived, something made her take her earphones off. She listened:

"If you really want to read Hemingway," someone was saying, "Ali al-Qassimi's translations are the way to go."

She lingered there awhile. The man who had just spoken was a very handsome and elegant young man. The more she looked at him, the more her arteries pulsed with strange celerity. *I think I'm in love.*

* * *

The next morning, she examined the place where her *Hemingway man* had been standing the other day. It was a small seafood restaurant, and nobody was there yet. Only a gray, lonely pigeon was searching for leftovers on the pavement. She made a mental note to look for her man on her way back.

And on her way back, it happened. At exactly five forty-one p.m., she spotted him again, inside the restaurant. Her entire body now pulsed with emotion, and she knew she was a slave to him forever.

The weekend marked three days since she'd confessed her feelings to herself, and she was determined to make a move. She dressed up and headed down to the seafood restaurant. She would order some fish and shrimp, she was thinking as she got there. Yet then, for the first time ever, she realized that the large blue sign atop the restaurant's door read:

THE OLD MAN AND THE SEA

She was nonplussed. The narrow entrance of the restaurant had led her into a magical bubble of sorts. Old Santiago was there in his small boat, and she went out with him to explore the sea…

And then her head turned. Slowly, she began to gaze at the figure behind the cash register. It was her Hemingway man!

Her heart bounced. Her nose had picked his scent from the countless smells of the restaurant: different types of smoked fish and frying oils. She was seasick. *Am I really with Santiago in his boat, and this is merely the scent of iodine from the sea?* she thought. *Or am I in the presence of my love in his strong-smelling restaurant at the corner of my street?*

Her brain received mixed signals. She was dizzy and soon passed out.

* * *

When she came to, the nurse at the nearby clinic was gazing down at her. That wasn't the interesting part, though; the interesting part was how her Hemingway man spoke then: wishing her a speedy recovery before excusing himself back to his restaurant.

He must have had some basic education, she thought, *but no more. Anyway, it doesn't matter. It's more than enough that he knows who Hemingway is and that he has a restaurant called "The Old Man and the Sea."*

But "The Old Man and the Sea" is not exactly how al-Qassimi has titled his famous translation, my dear, a voice said at the back of her head. *Al-Qassimi's translation is titled "The Sage and the Sea." This means that your "Hemingway man" has actually never read Hemingway.*

No. He's so handsome! she resisted. *He's so suave and kind, too. I think he is as good as it gets.*

She felt good about him and was sick no longer.

* * *

A week of fretting and sleepless nights then passed. She realized that she would never feel well if she did not confess her feelings to him. She read al-Qassimi's translation twice in two days, hoping for a way to get through to her love. But she did not find any. She could also not hold a clear picture of the "old man" in her head, nor imagine him talking to his oars or to his hands or to the barracuda fish or to the seabirds. She was very disappointed.

She believed she had caused the novel to lose its charm when she'd read it as a road map rather than a work of art, so she decided to read a different translation. She had an abridged version of the novel in her library, made for youths, but this one read so shallow and rawboned…just another thriller in the open seas. So she was now twice disappointed. She was actually in a sort of crisis. Losing faith in *The Old Man and the Sea* was tantamount to losing faith in the most beautiful thing in her life.

The next thing she did was call one of her literary friends. She besought her friend to be honest about his view of *The Old Man and the* Sea, and her friend said he believed this one novel wasn't the best of Hemingway; in his opinion, *A Moveable Feast* (which had an excellent translation by al-Qassimi, too) was the best thing Hemingway ever wrote.

Now she was seriously breaking down. She felt like she was giving up on all the good things in her life. She hung up on this friend of hers and spent the night curled up in bed, fetus-like, weeping.

* * *

The next day, when she walked by the restaurant, she noticed that her Hemingway man was paler than usual. His eyes were hollow, and his clothes and hair were unkempt and rumpled. A thought zipped through her head that *she* might be the reason for all this. Her love was suffering because she had lost her faith in *The Old Man and the Sea*. How beautiful her Hemingway man had looked back then, at the clinic, when he had said, "Get better soon, okay?"

She swallowed hard and felt bitter about it all. The bitterness grew in her mouth, in her throat. Soon seawater was gushing through her belly; she was drowning.

One thing saved her, though—and it was an elusive thought. *What if*, she thought, *what if I gave this novel a second chance as a movie?*

She sat down and watched the 1958 adaptation of the novel. But she found the visual effects primitive and could not stand Spencer Tracy's performance as "the old man." This made her disappointment grow even further. Ninety-five minutes had she wasted in front of the screen, only to realize that that adaptation was anything but honest.

She was getting more and more lost. Her night was rife with maddening visions.

* * *

The next day, she decided not to go to work. She didn't even bother with calling in. *Santiago was away at sea for a whole three days*, she thought. *No one judged him for it. No one demanded anything from him. The boy was caring for his shack in his absence, waiting for his return. Why would I need to account for my absence!*

At noon, she dressed up and made for the restaurant. She must see him, tell him how she felt. But maybe after she ate a dish of gray mullets with rice, salad, and tahini? She thought that might bolden her up before making her move.

She was wearing her sunglasses to avoid direct eye contact with him. She also took her time walking down the stairs. Once she was out of the building, she walked a hundred meters or so to the right—that was how far the seafood restaurant stood from her home—then she had to stop. Government cars were everywhere. Most belonged to the National Supply Authority, with Food Safety agents and some vets amongst them. The restaurant was being raided, being accused of selling seafood not fit for human consumption.

She would postpone her romantic plans for later, she decided. Yet just as she was turning away, she caught sight of her Hemingway man. How sickly he looked … how pallid. He even seemed to have lost some of his front hair as well. His rich eyebrows were now small, nothing like how she had remembered them, big like two great oars.

* * *

Guilt overtook her. She tried to think of a way to salvage whatever she could from the fray, but couldn't. She traced the recent events in her head, attempting to pinpoint the moment where chaos started. The way her Hemingway man had looked today, struggling to convince the government agents that he was doing nothing wrong, brought tears to her eyes. She blamed only herself. Could she go back in time to fix all this? If only she could change the past few days! She would never have removed her earphones to begin with. She would not have given him a glance. And she would guard her high opinion of *The Old Man and the Sea* with all her might.

If only…

* * *

On the tenth day of her Hemingway-man odyssey, a new idea popped into her head. She had no tasks nor chores that day, so why not reevaluate the novel by reading online reviews?

As she well knew, most readers did not bother with writing a review unless they had thoroughly enjoyed the book. Thus book reviews were mostly celebratory in nature, showering praise on all and sundry.

On one book-review website, she found three Arabic translations of the novel. The first was by a translator she did not know, and it was given four stars out of five. The second did not include the translator's name at all, and it boasted three stars. The last listing was the very abridged translation she possessed in her library. This one boasted a single star and had a written review, strangely in verse:

Poets are followed by simpletons;
Don't you see why they roam every valley?
They babble away and never do.

Reading that hurt her probably the most. She was discouraged from carrying on with her search. She was living in a closed-minded society, she realized. What was the point of anything!

She shut down her computer and headed out to her work, feeling stuck in the doldrums. Everything she'd ever wanted in life was a mere hundred meters away; yet she couldn't even confess her feelings to him, nor save him from decline.

* * *

She tried to look away from the restaurant when she walked by it, but she couldn't stop herself. A new sign was taped to the windowpane; it read:

FOR RENT

She dropped her purse. Inside the restaurant, her Hemingway man was giving orders to some workers, leaning on a pair of old crutches. *Did he just lose some of his teeth as well?* She was dazed and sweaty. It was as though unhappiness were growing in her gut like a tree… a tree with so many branches bursting out of her mouth, her nostrils, her ears, to cover the whole world.

* * *

She no longer kept count of days. On this one day, she got up earlier than usual, despite having gone through the worst night of her whole life. (She'd drowned in blue waters; the barracudas swallowed her up whole; she had even watched herself being crushed inside a giant book, like a withered rose.) It was still a bit after dawn. She made some tea, then emailed her resignation to her manager. Her misery had brimmed over and was about to overflow; she could not let that happen to her, never.

She went to the kitchen and grabbed the biggest metal pot she had. On the balcony, she tossed her two copies of *The Old Man and the Sea* in the pot and set them on fire. She watched the flames go through the pages slowly but fiercely. The strangest thing about it was how much smoke came out of the pot. The souls of Santiago, the boy, and all those species of fish were rising up to the heavens from her very balcony.

She poured water into the pot, then cleaned her balcony. She went back to her room, drew the curtains, powered off her cell phone, then descended into a long and deep sleep.

* * *

When she woke up, she didn't know how much time had passed. Being very hungry, she believed it must have been a whole day. She got dressed and made for the door, planning to buy some food. But as she opened her front door, she was astonished to find an electricity bill taped there, on the outside. *This can't be unless I have been asleep for at least a couple of days*, she thought. She slipped the bill in her purse and climbed down the stairs. Once she was out of the building, she turned right—as she always did.

As she came level with where the seafood restaurant was supposed to be, she was forced to stop. *The Old Man and the Sea* was nowhere to be seen, and a different kind of shop stood in its place. This one had a cornucopia of smoking gear—shisha bowls, trays, and different types of hoses—crammed in its front. The sign over its door was red and glossy, reading, in glaring white:

THE TOBACCO SHOP

OWNED BY

MR. PESSOA

Camphor Forestland

By **Said Takieddine**, translated by **Dima El-Mouallem**

No, no, my friend. Here I am, and here I will stay. You might wonder about the reason that made me a recluse who's afraid of seeing people. Berate me all you like, wax poetic about the beauty of this life all you like. You won't tempt me to leave the house. I know how mesmerizing the suburbs are, but good luck getting me out of this chair. Ah, I aroused your curiosity? Very well; I owe it to you to divulge my secret, then. My love of seclusion is no mystery, really. It was a result of a little promenade I went on last year, on a night just like this, in the suburbs of the city.

It was after sundown, that solitary hour. I shot out of the house and drove my car to the suburbs. When I got to the spot where the road grows wide and the houses grow massive and tall, I continued on foot, walking lazily and observing the mansions—the Suburb of Millions, they call it. These millions rose up as skyscraping trees, lay flat as rose gardens, and stood proud as marble columns. As night fell, the glow of electric lights came about, then a deafening roar came out of the throats of phonographs and radios.

My greatest wonder, however, was caused by the names written in light at the entrances of these mansions, announcing their owners. It was as though the proprietors were not content to revel in luxury if they could not announce that they, and not some other people, were the inhabitants of paradise. Besides, a person tends to be enamored with their own name. Do you want to become a rich man and live in the suburbs yourself? All you have to do is invent a machine that engraves a person's name on their forehead in neon letters without causing them harm. Here, light a cigarette. Don't yawn like that. The story I'm about to tell you will shake you to the core. I'll go on telling it right now without any philosophizing whatsoever.

I continued my leisurely walk until my eyes came upon the name on the gate of "Villa of Remondo Topacio." Well, well! So that's where our friend Remondo was living, or rather hiding. Remondo, whom people once called The Volcano.

I found myself at the gate below two lines of neon, before a rampart-like concierge who flaunted a tuxedo, asking him to tell Remondo that I'd like to come inside.

The concierge was disgusted by my tone and my asking after his master by his first name, for debasing the master humiliates his help. But forgive *me*; I promised not to philosophize! Oh, look: your cigarette went out. Go ahead and light it; the matchbox is on your right.

As I was saying, the concierge was disgruntled, so he lifted his snout up to the heavens and raised through it a storm of air that puffed up his chest, a storm that he presently huffed in my face. He said, "I'll go see whether Don—*Don*!— Remondo is within."

As I observed the Rampart advance toward the mansion to announce my name to his master, I remembered a thousand things about Remondo. Remondo used to write a column in a daily, entitled 'The Fire of the Lake.' They called him the Volcano because his ink was lava and his tongue was fire.

Like everyone else, I, too, read his daily article and delighted in it. Besides that, I knew him well at the personal level. I admired his worn clothes and the poverty that clung to him without vanquishing his spirit. I remember one night I was in some nightclub. It was late. The attendant gave me a bill of about fifty riyals, within which was enclosed a paper that read:

"My Friend,

A ravishing blonde is in my arms and I find myself positively unable to reach my pocket. Here's the bill: either pay it or tell the waiter to eat it!

The Volcano"

Of course, I paid the bill. I kept the invoice, too. Who knows? This promenade just might give me back fifty riyals that were, to me, as good as lost.

Presently, the Rampart returned. He bowed before me respectfully and invited "the gentleman" to honor the mansion with his presence, for the master was on the second-floor veranda that looked out to the sea.

I swear: if I hadn't known Remondo well, I wouldn't have dared to trespass on that paradise of stone, nor to tramp on its carpets.

If servants hadn't appeared at every new turn to show me the way to go and the right stairs to climb, I would've lost my way among those feathers, oil paintings, and artworks.

And yet, a deafening silence that ricocheted everywhere in the mansion made my hair stand on end. I heard neither laughter nor yelling, no radio droned, no lady spoke, no children fought.

These swift and horrifying thoughts left me completely as I went out to the veranda and saw the most beautiful view in my life. I heard Remondo welcoming me, so I said, "Hello there, Volcano!"

Remondo laughed and opened his mouth to say, "Ah. The Volcano. I believe you're back to claim your fifty riyals. Rest assured, you'll have them, but sit down first. Do you prefer that we turn on the lights, or would you rather, as I do, relish this divine view? Look out to the sea and listen to its susurrus. Here are the fishermen's boats. Look. Do you see the fire that's blazing about their oars? In this spot out at sea, the phosphorus glows in the water."

I asked, "So that's 'The Fire of the Lake'? Indeed, I prefer it to electric lights." I sat down and he took a seat at a distance from me, at the farthest end of the veranda.

It was eerie how the two of us went quiet in the darkness of that veranda.

Being my host, it seemed that he felt awkward about the silence, so he took to pressing his buzzer. Servants manifested, carrying trays and all manner of food and drink. Afterward, he would revert to pointing out the wondrousness of the sea view and the crescent peeping through the clouds.

Perhaps the scotch loosened my tongue and forced an insolent question from it, as I yelled at my companion, "To hell with the crescent, the sea, the boats, and fishermen! Explain this mystery to me: the mansion, your seclusion, 'The Fire of the Lake' that went out, and the volcano that became dormant …"

Remondo replied, "I'll open up to you if I can manage it. I feel rigid with stupefaction. Perhaps if I revolted just once and divulged my secret, I would regain something of my conscious feeling and liveliness. Well, you remember that I was a writer in a newspaper. You read me, as did a hundred thousand others. You met me, like others did, with smiles and banter and friendly looks. I had been but a boy in the battle we call life, and I didn't go through it like a soldier but like a gang that struck, spreading tyranny every which way, mocking everyone and everything.

"Four hundred riyals: that was my salary. I got it in the morning, at the end of every month, and distributed it that same afternoon amongst my creditors—or some of them, at least. I can't recall one single marketplace that didn't have at least one shop with my name down in its ledger of debts. Never could I be part of a crowd that was entirely free of my creditors. You remember my radio broadcasts, which I began with, 'Dear friends and creditors.'

"And yet, I was neither thief nor conman: I organized my debts meticulously. Whatever got paid at the end of the month was a settled debt, and whatever was still around the following month was a debt deferred.

"More than a hundred letters came in the mail each day: encouragements and threats, love letters and threatening letters. Cab drivers vied to give me free rides, and many a time did I eat at a restaurant and ask for the check only for the owner to smile and say it was on the house.

"Many were the times that I sat drinking in the club only for a bottle of champagne to appear at my table with a white card that read, 'from an admiring fan.' As for admirers of the opposite sex, well, some Ottoman sultan might've matched me in the number of his concubines, but *my* harem didn't cost me a single riyal.

"Government officials and industrial magnates? I was their bane. Nary a man had strayed from the straight path except that he saw his guts splattered on the pages of my daily column.

"You remember my crusade against the Minister of the Navy. Who didn't read about 'the fleet of dryland' and 'the admiral of the swimming pool?' Who didn't enjoy my description of the 'aged armored cruiser' or of the Minister of the Navy and his breakneck warship of a wife? Ah, you giggle, so you remember. Surely you remember the submarine, too.

"At the height of my crusade against the minister, my phone rang, and His Excellency was at the other end. He spoke in soft tones and honeyed words, begging me to go over and meet him. I asked, 'And the cab fare?' He said that his personal car was at the paper's door. And what do you know, I peaked out of the window and there was his blue automobile: blue like the sea, blue like the Navy.

"As I dove into that atlas of a car, I thought of a thousand jokes and a thousand articles about this visit.

"When I entered into the presence of the minister, I descried smiles in the eyes of his aides. As I sat, listening to him, I felt like a mouse being toyed with by a cat. Every second I expected that he would rip me to shreds.

"Nevertheless, the gentility persisted. He took to calling me son."

"Son, you're a quick, clever boy. I'm proud of you. This country needs volcanoes like you. Don't you think that I resent you, son. I like criticism, I encourage it even. We're only human, and to err is human. It's no less than your journalistic duty to point out our blunders to us. So what if you mention said mistakes using a comic style and caustic expressions? You end your articles with a 'Crack!' That explosive firecracker of a word that precedes your signature. Isn't that so, son? I suppose you can't stand praise. You must be sick of people fawning over you. I didn't invite you here, anyway, to laud your manners and your journalistic genius. I invited you here to let you in on a venture. You know that the Ministry of the Navy is the custodian of the state's forests spanning tens of thousands of hectares filled with giant trees whose age heaven only knows, and whose timber we use to manufacture our ships.

"Not all of these forests are fit for ship-making, and it's a crime for them to lie fallow. The law, son, allows any citizen to own ten thousand hectares as long as he's the first to file a claim, provided that we had already announced that the trees in those forests are not fit for ship-making. Son, I would love for you to file a claim to become the owner of a forest of camphor trees, the one we call 'Camphor Forestland.'

"Camphor, as you know, is used to make boxes, not ships. *You* can't invest in this forest, but an American company stands ready to rent it from you. Son, you know that the law prohibits leasing state property to foreign companies, but they can cooperate with you to benefit from the forest. The truth is, the company representative is in the outer office right this minute, and he's willing to sign an agreement with you that brings you fifty grand a year. This way, you fill your own pockets, you fill the state's treasury through the profits we'll be making in taxes, and you provide a living to thousands of workers and contractors.

"Just sign this petition, son. I would never want to encroach on your idealistic tendencies, so keep working hard at your job, and let your lava flow free, Volcano!'"

"I signed.

"The next day, I went to the office as was my habit every morning. I sat down to write down my daily piece, and I was horrified to find that my mind was blank. After strenuous effort, I managed to push an article onto the desk of the old typesetter who reads the text before arranging it. I was astounded, for he asked me, for the first time ever, to read out a few words that he couldn't decipher himself. Shortly after, he came up to my desk in his ink-splotched clothes, and said with a smile on his face, 'You forgot something, sir. Where's the whip-crack at the end of the article?'

"My daily mail dried up little by little until it became so meager that I only got one or two letters a week. The editor was on my back. One morning, he passed by my desk; he read my article then tore it up, and advised me, derisively, to restrict myself to writing about the weather from now on.

"During that period, the paperwork for Camphor Forestland was completed, and I got paid. I quit my job at the paper and began building this mansion.

"Do you know the reason for my seclusion? Now you'll see, you'll see with your own eyes. Come here, come closer to this lamp. It's shining brightly, so come closer and take a look at my face. Stare, I tell you!"

He grabbed my arm and moved his face closer to the lamp. He growled, "I said stare, so stare! Can't you see the trees etched on my countenance? Speak! Can't you see Camphor Forestland on my face?

Upon my honor, I did stare, and I saw the forest traced on Remondo's visage. Trembling, I said, "I see it. I see it!" He yelled at me again, "Now, get a whiff of this! Smell! Can't you smell the camphor wafting from me? Answer me! Answer me, I say!"

I closed my eyes and inhaled deeply. I swear that I smelled camphor.

Again, he squawked, "I spend my days upon this darkened veranda so that people won't be able to see Camphor Forestland in my face. I sat so far away from you so you couldn't detect the smell of the camphor that's embalming my body. I am the corpse of the Volcano, disfigured and embalmed."

I pried myself loose from Remondo's arms and leaped out of the mansion, going out the gate after pushing the Rampart aside.

It wasn't Remondo's calamity that caused my isolation. After all, Remondo wasn't exactly my friend, although I did like him. What caused this seclusion of mine was that after that fateful visit to the mansion, I took to studying people's faces, and I saw Camphor Forestland in each face. I listened closely, and I smelled the odor of camphor engulfing their bodies and embalming them. No, no, my friend. Here I am, and here I will stay. Wax poetic about the beauty of this life all you like. You won't tempt *me* to visit the suburbs. Your cigarette went out again. Go ahead and light it; the matchbox is on your right.

Read & Eat

'Mother of Happy Endings' & the Indian Mirror

By **Nawal Nasrallah**

It sounded very much like shooting in the dark when Marcia asked if, for the upcoming theme of 'Mirrors,' I knew of "any sort of recipe or food that would fit this." "Or is that a silly question?" she hastened to add.

Photo: Anny Gaul

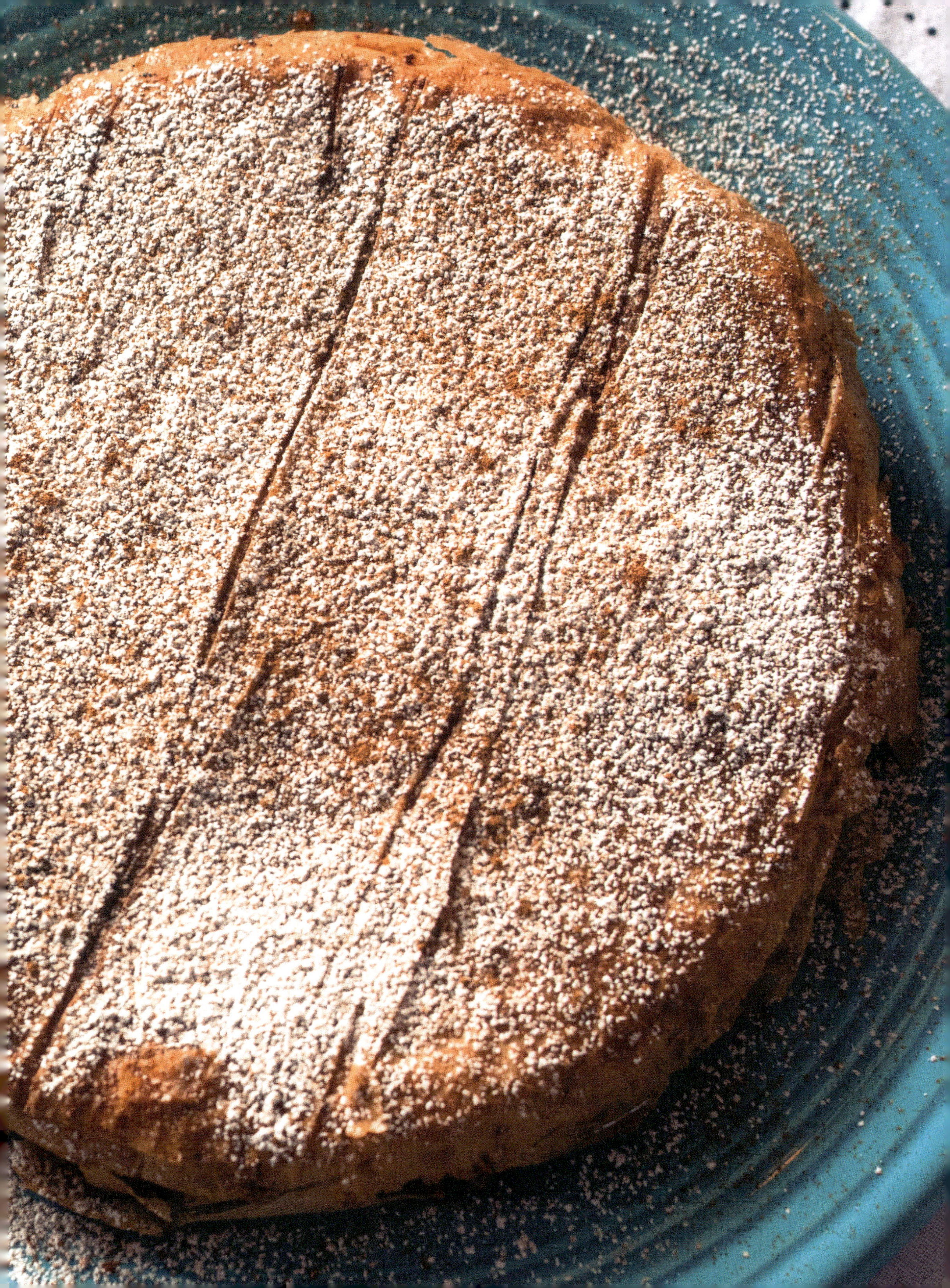

The question in fact could not have been timelier, as I was at the time in the middle of translating a thirteenth-century Andalusi text and trying to wrap my head around a recipe in which ultra-thin sheets of pastry are intriguingly baked on a gadget the recipe called *mir'at Hindiyya* (Indian mirror). These sheets of bread, called *ruqaq*, were required for making an extraordinarily exquisite and elaborate sweet-savory chicken pie, which the recipe nicknamed *Umm al-Faraj*: "Mother of Happy Endings." Giving nicknames to dishes was a common practice in medieval times, such as calling wheat porridge *Umm al-Khayr* (Mother of Plenty), or fine white bread *Abu Badr* (Father of the Full Moon). *Umm al-Faraj* was undoubtedly meant to be a playful commentary on a complex and labor-intensive dish that resulted in a magnificent "bundle of joy," profusely described at the end of the recipe as remarkably delicious and aromatic, fit for no less than kings.

According to the recipe, the cook is directed to heat up this so-called *mir'at Hindiyya* on a coal fire and, once it gets hot, it is held by the handle right above a bowl containing the prepared flour-based batter. The batter is poured onto the face of the mirror so that it coats it entirely, and whatever does not stick will fall back into the bowl, leaving a very thin coating on the mirror, which the recipe compares to *ghilala* (sheer cloth). The resulting pastry is shaken off onto a piece of cloth, and the procedure is repeated as many times as needed.

For those familiar with today's North African festive sweet and savory bird pie *bastīla* (bastilla), which defines the region's culinary refinement, the similarities between today's dish—with its ultra-thin sheets of pastry, the *warqa* or *malsuqa*—and *Umm al-Faraj* cannot be missed, as indeed we see in it the earliest surviving precursor.[1]

Now the question is: What sort of mirror was it that the medieval cooks used, and for what purpose? Was it an actual mirror, and, if so, what was it made of, and why Indian of all possible mirrors? To us modern cooks, baking on mirrors is a foreign concept, as it was, it seems, to the scribe of the seventeenth-century manuscript of the cookbook where the recipe is found,[2] for at the place where '*mir'at Hindiyya*' occurs, we can clearly see the word *kadha* كذا (sic) jotted down directly above. However, judging from references to it in records contemporaneous with the time of our book or thereabouts, the Indian mirror seemed to have been a familiar item. We read, for instance, that when the Andalusi Arab traveler Ibn Jubayr (d. 1217) visited the famous shrine in Cairo where the head of the Prophet's grandson al-Husayn was buried, he marveled at a glistening black stone wall that reflected the visitors' images, which he compared to a newly polished Indian mirror.[3] In his book on interpretations of dreams, Ibn Shahin (d. 1468) considers it a bad omen to see oneself in a dream looking into an Indian mirror,[4] a clear indication that it was an easily recognized household object. The mirror's capacity for reflecting intense heat, causing fires, was also demonstrated in a verse line attributed to the eleventh-century Cordovan poet Ibn Hananiya (Ibn al-Hannat):

If you only knew of the fire already raging in my heart,
You wouldn't have had to light it with Indian mirrors and bitumen.[5]

---

[1] For a discussion on etymological possibilities and other aspects of the bastilla dish, see: http://www.cliffordawright.com/caw/food/entries/display.php/topic_id/3/id/66/, accessed Jan. 25, 2022.
See also Anny Gaul's post, "Seven Centuries Bstila": https://cookingwithgaul.com/2018/02/25/seven-centuries-of-bstila/, accessed Jan. 25, 2022.

[2] Anonymous, *Anwa' al-saydala fi alwan al-at'ima*; English translation forthcoming.

[3] *Rihlat Ibn Jubayr*, edited by Karam al-Bustani, Beirut: 1964.

[4] Ibn Shahin, *al-Isharat fi 'ilm al-'ibarat*, edited by Sayyid Hasan, Beirut: 1993.

[5] The Indian mirror is here referred to as al-Hindi, which may also associate it with excellent swords made in India, or Indian aloeswood. However, yoking it here with bitumen would rule out such possibilities.

Sundari, or "Lady with the Mirror," is carved on wall of Belur Temple in the Hassan district of Karnataka state, India. © WikiCommons

The medieval Arabic lexicons are not much of help in this regard; there is only mention of swords called *Hindi* and *muhannad*, designated good-quality Indian swords made with the good iron from India. Modern histories on the development of the manufacturing of mirrors point to the fact that mirrors were made of metal everywhere from ancient times and up to around the sixteenth century, when both steel and glass mirrors were used, but glass eventually dominated, from the seventeenth century.[6] Therefore, mirrors during medieval times, Indian or otherwise, had to be metal ones, and if they were described as Hindi, then they might well have been made with good Indian iron. But what was good Indian iron?

The answer to this is found in a medieval treatise, a unique volume on mineralogy, *al-Jamahir fi ma'rifat al-jawahir*, by al-Biruni (d. ca. 1050), where, in his section on iron,[7] differences among varieties of this metal are explained:

1) *Narmahin*, which is wrought iron, known to be low in carbon content, is described as feminine on account of its softness and malleability.

2) *Dus*, which is cast iron, is known for its high carbon content. It is also called *ma' al-hadid*, or "water of iron," which al-Biruni describes as the liquid that separates and is the first to flow when iron ore is smelted to

[6] *See, for instance, Sabine Melchior-Bonnet, The Mirror: A History, English translation: 2001.*

[7] *Al-Biruni, al-Jamahir fi ma'rifat al-jawahir, edited by Yusuf al-Hadi, Tehran: 1995, pp. 404–14.*

الخبز الصالح للحم [...] قدر الكبة يه وبو [...] مع حبوب وكمام عش ببهار
ويبرد ولا يغسل بحر [...] يفشع زيته ويلتثم [...] معه ثم يبرز ويسخ ويستخ
مثل العصيدة بعد ما يهم رعبا من السكر العصفور وما ادرت من انواع الدسم وطاط هار

عصيدة ممششة

تحذى وتسمن يؤخذ وجه من افخم الجشر
اللحم كورا ويصب عليه غم ما ويطبخ حتى يجف الما ثم يسقى بالبر الحليب ويبرز
ثم يضاف اليه عسل من زوع الزغرة ومرج مع اللحم المطبوخ مع شحمه
ساد عليه مرات حتى يعجنة ثم تلف عليه زبدة طربا وسكرا مع فوفا وباتيج ابيضا
رشويه مسحوقة ويفح به انه نور طيب و

ذكر انواع الرييس واطعمة الخبز والحلاوه

صنعة عمل الجوذابه

وتسمى الفرج وهو طعام مش[ـ]
يؤخذ من شحم الخلا[ـ] الغنم والمعز المنفا السمين من غشيته وعروفه وبه وجه منه
حج او عمود ذا ناعما حتى يصير مثل الدماع ثم يخذ فدر جديد ويعد خلاط الشحم بالبه
ويطلى به داخل الفدر كله فرا وجوانبا حتى يكون عليه غلظ لا يصبع له يؤخذ
الرقلو المصنوع على المراة رغبا حما حافي مشا ترة و حما طار يعجر العجين مما اد رما
ويج مركبه على صفة المشعدة ليلا يتلم بيه غرا حمو يصب للبلا شيا بعد شيا حتى
يؤفه الحسوم تخشي مراة هندية على نار لحم مدته له باذ احمت مسكت على جعه
العجير مبللة وصب عليها الكاسا الكاس حتى يجمع معها ويعاد العجير الى الجعنة وفه على بالمروا
غلالة رقيقة بذ لط عواو فا وبه الكد[ـ]واده وتنفض على منديل فيخرج مستديرة على شد
المراة ثم يصب من العجير كما بعد ا ولا حتى يجمع منه فدر الحل جمة ثم يوخذ مما جا
اسمار البتية تنطع وسوع[ـ]ع ورما وجعل[ـ]رة فدر كعاف كعاها وباضا اثم[ـ]
ورد[ـ] ولقارف[ـ] ومسبا[ـ] وبرع على النار وتصبح حتى تنضج باذ[ـ]واحد[ـ] الخ[ـ]

extract the base metal (wrought iron). When this so-called "iron water" separates, it is collected as cast iron, which al-Biruni describes as *sulb,* "hard iron." This is silvery white in hue, unmalleable, and hence susceptible to breakage when hammered.

3) *Shaburqan,* which is meteoritic iron, is called masculine on account of its hard nature. Al-Biruni says this variety is rare.

In addition to the above, al-Biruni discusses how a manufactured type of iron (*masnu'*) was produced by combining wrought iron (*narmahin*) with cast iron ("water of iron," *dus*), resulting in *fuladh,* which is steel. Al-Biruni further explains that this steel is molded in crucibles into egglike pieces (*bayd,* sg. *bayda*), elongated with rounded bases, commonly compared to ostrich eggs (*bayd al-ni'am*). And that was how the manufactured pieces of steel acquired the name "ostrich eggs," or just "eggs."

Besides the above-mentioned method followed in producing steel in crucibles, two other procedures were also common, as Egyptian alchemist al-Jildaki (d. 1342) explains, copying from *Kitab al-Hadid* (*A Book on Iron*) by his predecessor, the Arab scientist Jabir b. Hayyan (d. 815): [8]

8 *As mentioned in Hassan and Hill, Islamic Technology, Paris: 1986.*

Either cast iron was given some malleability by decarbonating it to make steel, or wrought iron was made a bit harder by carbonating it, after which the resulting refined steel was left to harden into "ostrich eggs;" and it was in this form that manufactured steel was widely traded in the medieval Muslim world. As al-Biruni attests, India was reputed for making the best of swords, helmets, and other items with steel, which was imported from steel-manufacturing centers in Herat (in eastern Afghanistan) and even from as far-off a place as al-Maghrib.

And so it was from this steel, *fuladh,* that the famed Indian objects were made and exported far and wide, including their fine steel mirrors. In fact, to this day metal mirrors are still being handcrafted on a very small scale in Aranmula, a small town in Kerala, India. As you might expect, the steel Indian mirrors made to function as a kitchen gadget—as used in the Andalusi recipe—and not as an ordinary mirror, must have been polished into a mirror finish, and hence the name. Their extremely polished surfaces offered excellent nonstick properties and were the best to use for such a delicate task as baking sheets of pastry as thin as sheer fabric.

Opposite page
Fol. 62r from MS. Arabe 7009 of Anwa' al-saydala, where the word kadha (sic) is written on the sixth line from the bottom
©BNF

Now to our precursor of the modern-day *bastila,* the savory-sweet chicken pie, *Umm al-Faraj,* which the recipe also considered as a variety of *judhaba.* As early as the ninth century, the original *judhaba* as it was prepared in the eastern region, al-Mashriq, was composed of two parts: 1) the pan in which a sweet preparation, often composed of layered paper-thin breads drenched in syrup, placed on the floor of a preheated clay oven, *tannur,* and 2) the skewered large chunk of meat, which could be a lamb, a chicken, a duck, and the like, left suspended above the bread pan to receive its drippings. By the thirteenth century, as *Umm al-Faraj* clearly demonstrates, it seems that the Andalusi cooks had already taken the *judhaba* a step further by combining the meat and the pastry part into a "bundle of joy."

A *judhaba* dish called *Umm al-Faraj* (Mother of Happy Endings): [9]

[9] Anonymous, *Anwa' al-saydala fi alwan al-at'ima*; English translation forthcoming.

Note in case you feel like trying the dish: If you happen to own one of those expensive mirror polished metal pans, go ahead and use it, just remember not to see your face in it in your dreams. Otherwise, a good nonstick pancake pan will work just fine.

Take suet from the kidneys of fat sheep or goats, cleaned of its membranes and veins, and pound it in a mortar of stone or wood thoroughly into a brain-like consistency. Take a new pot and, after pressing and kneading the suet by hand, smear the entire inside of the pot with it—base and sides—to the thickness of one finger.

Now, take thin discs of baked bread; here is how to make them: First make dough with fine white flour, press and knead it vigorously, then start thinning it gradually with water [and kneading it] until it becomes as thin as soup.

Heat up a *mir'at Hindiyya* (Indian mirror) on a moderately burning coal fire, and, once it gets hot, wet it, and hold it vertically [from its handle] above the batter bowl. Scoop the batter with a glass and pour it on the [surface of the] mirror until it is entirely coated with it. The batter will fall back into the bowl, leaving a very thin layer on the mirror, like *ghilala* (sheer cloth); and this will be your thin bread. Shake it onto a clean piece of cloth, and it will look as round as the mirror itself. Repeat pouring the batter [on the heated, wet mirror] as done above until you collect the needed amount of pastry sheets.

Take fat young-adult chickens, clean them, and cut open their chests [to flatten them]. Put them in a pot as they are, whole, with salt, olive oil, black pepper, Ceylon cinnamon (*qirfa*), and spikenard (*sunbul*). Put the pot on the fire until the chicken cooks and all the pot's liquid has dried out.

Now, take two of the prepared breads and line the bottom and sides of the prepared pot with them; let their ends hang down from the pot. Sprinkle them with coarsely crushed sugar, skinned almonds, spikenard, cassia (*dar Sini*), and cloves (*qaranful*)—what amounts to one ladleful. Drizzle sweet olive oil all over them, and sprinkle with rosewater in which a small amount of musk and camphor have been dissolved—add enough to moisten the sugar. Next, spread two more sheets of bread, sprinkle them as was first done, with sugar, almonds, spices, and olive oil, and sprinkle all with rosewater; then spread other sheets of bread, and repeat. Continue doing this until half of the pot is filled.

Take the prepared cooked chickens, rub them with saffron dissolved in rosewater, and arrange them on the [layered] bread in the pan. Once more, cover them with more of the bread, sprinkle them with sugar, almonds, and spices as was done before, and continue doing this until the pot is full, with the chickens buried in the middle.

Once all this is done, sprinkle the top with lots of sugar, pour olive oil and rosewater all over, and cover it with the bread ends left hanging from the sides. Cover the pot with a lid tightly fastened to it with some dough. Place it in a moderately hot brick oven (*furn*), and leave it there for the same amount of time that it takes meat to cook in a pot.

When you take the pot out of the oven and break the seal, it will emit a fragrant aroma. Discard the burnt layers of bread, if any, and turn it over—as it is in one piece—onto a vessel large enough to contain it, and present it. It is a remarkably delicious and aromatic dish, fit for kings.

Best of Delectable Foods and Dishes from al-Andalus and al-Maghrib

A Cookbook by Thirteenth-Century Andalusi Scholar Ibn Razīn al-Tujībī (1227–1293)

English Translation with Introduction and Glossary

BY
NAWAL NASRALLAH

ISLAMIC HISTORY AND CIVILIZATION: STUDIES AND TEXTS

BRILL

The middle jewel in the "**unique necklace**" of medieval Arabic cookery books that survived from the eastern and western regions of the Arabo-Muslim world.

This thirteenth-century cookbook by the Andalusi scholar Ibn Razīn al-Tujībī showcases the sophisticated cuisine that developed in the Iberian Peninsula when it was under Muslim rule, with its 475 delectable recipes, masterfully structured and explained.

Here, published for the first time in English, it presents al-Tujībī's complete text, based not only on the partial Berlin and Madrid manuscripts, but also on a newly discovered complete manuscript, now available for the first time in print format.

More at
theandalusikitchen.wordpress.com.

BRILL

Contributors

A

Rasha Abbas is a Syrian journalist and writer of short stories. She is currently based in Berlin, Germany. In 2008, she published her first collection, *Adam Hates the Television*, and was awarded a prize for young writers during the Damascus Capital of Arab Culture festival. In 2013 she co-wrote the script for a short film, *Happiness and Bliss*, produced by Bedayat, and in 2014 she contributed, both as a writer and as a translator, to *Syria Speaks: Art and Culture from the Frontline*, published by Saqi Books. Her second short story collection, *The Gist of It*, was published in 2019.

Reem Abbas is a multilingual poet, poetry critic, and reviewer. She has published poems with the PNR and PBRUM, and is currently an Undertow poet at the Poetry Translation Centre. She has reviewed or is currently reviewing poetry collections for various literary journals. She is also writing her PhD at the University of Cambridge on Persian influences in Basil Bunting's poetry.

Ra'ad Abdulqadir (1953–2003) was a pioneer of the Iraqi prose poem, the author of five poetry collections, and a lifelong editor of *Aqlam*, Iraq's leading literary magazine. *Except for This Unseen Thread: Selected Poems* (Ugly Duckling Presse), translated by Mona Kareem, is his first collection in English translation.

Sara Abou Rashed is a Palestinian American poet and speaker. She was born and raised in Syria, but has lived in the United States since 2013. At 16, Sara delivered a TEDxTalk and was nominated for a Pushcart Prize. Her works have appeared in the anthology *A Land With A People* and 9–12 Language Arts curriculum from McGraw Hill, and are forthcoming in *Poetry* magazine. In 2018, Sara launched her autobiographical one-woman show, *A Map of Myself*. She is currently a MFA candidate at the University of Michigan.

Karima Ahdad is a Moroccan writer, journalist, and author from the city of El Hoceima who worked until May 2021 as a digital content editor for TRT Arabi in Turkey. Her first novel, *Cactus Girls*, was published in 2018 and won the 2019 Mohamed Zefzaf prize. Her 2014 short story collection *The Last Hemorrhage of the Dream* was awarded the prize for best young author from the Moroccan Writers' Union. Ahdad has just completed a novel about Arabs living in Turkey. She speaks Arabic, French, English, and Amazigh.

Ali Jaafar Al Allaq is an Iraqi poet and academic who is the editor-in-chief of Iraqi literary magazine *al-Aqlam*. He has published twelve collections of poetry and multiple works of literary criticism while also serving as a jury member for many Arabic poetry and criticism awards.

Layla AlAmmar is a writer and academic from Kuwait. She has an MSc in Creative Writing from the University of Edinburgh. Her short stories have appeared in the *Evening Standard*, *Quail Bell Magazine*, the *St Andrews University Prose Journal*, and *Aesthetica Magazine*, where her story "The Lagoon" was a finalist for the 2014 Creative Writing Award. She was the 2018 British Council International Writer in Residence at the Small Wonder Short Story Festival. Her debut, *The Pact We Made*, was longlisted for the Authors' Club Best First Novel Award. Her second novel, *Silence is a Sense*, was published in Spring 2021. She has written for *The Guardian*, *LitHub*, the *Times Literary Supplement*, and *ArabLit Quarterly*. She is currently pursuing a PhD on the intersection of Arab women's fiction and literary trauma theory.

Ghada Alatrash, PhD, is an Assistant Professor in the School of Critical and Creative Studies at Alberta University of the Arts in Calgary, Canada. She holds a PhD in Educational Research: Languages and Diversity from the Werklund School of Education, the University of Calgary, and a Master's Degree in English Literature from the University of Oklahoma. Her current research speaks to Syrian art and creative expression as resistance to oppression and dictatorship.

Mustafa Taj Aldeen Almosa is a Syrian author and playwright. He has published six collections of short stories and four plays that have won him prestigious literary prizes in Syria and the Arab world. Several of his short stories have been translated into many European languages as well as Turkish, Japanese, Persian, and Kurdish.

Abdalrahman Alqalaq is a Palestinian poet and artist born and raised in Syria. His writings appear in numerous Arabic journals and his debut poetry collection titled *24* was released in 2022 from the Cairo-based publishing house, elles. He currently lives in Germany and studies theater at the University of Hildesheim.

Shahd Alshammari is Assistant Professor of Literature and the author of *Head Above Water: Reflections on Illness* (Neem Tree Press, London, 2022). She blogs at www.drshahdalshammari.com and is interested in disability studies, women's studies, and Arab women's literature.

Hilal Badr is the pen name of a Syrian poet.

Nawara Belal is an Egyptian feminist of color. She has been part of the Egyptian civil society, cultural and contemporary art scene, and feminist movement since 2010. Her interests and career have focused on social causes and using artistic tools of expression and public spaces. She also translates and edits, and her passion is bilingual poetry. She co-edited an artistic book on the different forms of imprisonment, *If Not For That Wall*, with CiC (Contemporary Image Collective) in 2018.

Mohamed Choukri (1935–2003) was a Moroccan writer and the author of novels like *Streetwise*, *Jean Genet and Tennessee Williams in Tanger*, and, most famously, *For Bread Alone*. He also wrote two collections of short stories, *Flower Crazy* and *The Tent*, that are forthcoming in Jonas Elbousty's translation.

Madeline Edwards is an editor, translator, occasional reporter, and book lover living in Beirut. She is the English editor of *SyriaUntold*, a nonprofit news organization focusing on arts, culture, and society in Syria and the diaspora. She is grateful to writer Haifa Abul-Nadi for sending her Maheera Migdadi's short story.

Jonas Elbousty holds an MPhil and PhD in English Studies from Columbia University. He is a writer, a literary translator, and an academic. He is the (co) author of three books, and his work has appeared (or is forthcoming) in *ArabLit, ArabLit Quarterly, Asheville Poetry Review, Banipal, Michigan Quarterly Review, Prospectus, Sekka, The Journal of North African Studies, International Journal of Middle East Studies,* and other venues. His translation of Mohamed Choukri's two short story collections, *Flower Crazy* and *The Tent*, is forthcoming from Yale University Press.

Dima El-Mouallem is a translator and a scholar of Islamic Studies. She earned her MA in Islamic Studies from the American University of Beirut, with a focus on the wonderful, the strange, and the miraculous.

Enas El-Torky graduated from the department of English language and literature at Ain Shams University, where she earned her PhD. She has published several translations and was shortlisted for the ArabLit Story Prize.

Zeena Faulk is an American-Iraqi literary translator and a PhD candidate in Translation Studies at the University of Warwick. Her translated works have appeared in *Banipal, ArabLit Quarterly*, and *Passa Porta*, among others.

Ibrahim Fawzy is an assistant lecturer and emerging translator from Egypt. He has a master's degree in comparative literature from Fayoum University in Egypt. His translations have appeared in *ArabLit, Merit Cultural Magazine, African Qira'at,* and *Sard Adabi*. He has published a number of academic articles. His first academic book, *Belonging to Prison*, is forthcoming in 2022.

Duna Ghali is a Danish-Iraqi novelist, poet, and translator born in Basra, Iraq. She graduated from the University of Basrah College of Agriculture in 1987 and has lived in Denmark since 1992. Ghali has published several novels, collections of poetry, and prose in Arabic, most notably the novels *The Further Point* (2000), *When the Scent Awakens* (2006), and *Orbits of Loneliness* (2014). Her most recent works in Arabic are *Never Tell Stories on Wednesdays* (2016), a collection of prose, and the novel *His Safe Haven* (2017). A collection of prose, *Behind a Mask*, will be published in spring 2022. Ghali has also published a novel and a collection of poetry in Danish, as well as a bilingual (Danish-Arabic) collection of prose.

Katharine Halls is an Arabic-to-English translator from Cardiff, Wales. She was awarded a 2021 PEN/Heim Translation Fund Grant for her translation of Haytham El-Wardany's *Things That Can't Be Fixed* and her translation, with Adam Talib, of Raja Alem's *The Dove's Necklace* received the 2017 Sheikh Hamad Award and was shortlisted for the Saif Ghobash Banipal Prize. Her translations for the stage have been performed at the Royal Court and the Edinburgh Festival, and short texts have appeared in *World Literature Today, Asymptote, Words Without Borders, Adda, Africa is A Country, Newfound, Critical Muslim, The Common, Arts of the Working Classes,* and various anthologies.

Ahmed Magdy Hammam, born in 1983, is an Egyptian journalist and author, and his short-story collection *The Gentleman Prefers Lost Causes* won the Sawiris Cultural Award in 2016. He was also shortlisted for the Asfari Award, organized by the American University in Beirut, in 2019. He lives in Cairo and works as a journalist and editor for *Al-Dostor* newspaper.

Burnaby Hawkes is an Egyptian-Canadian novelist, translator, and former political analyst for the NATO Council. He has two Arabic novels published in 2011 and 2020 (Merit Publishing House, Cairo), but now writes exclusively in English. His website is at www.burnabyhawkes.com.

Rema Hmoud is a Jordanian writer who lives in Kuwait and works as a teacher of Arabic. She is author of three novels and two short-story collections.

Alice Holttum is a part-time freelance translator and translation proofreader. She was born in Edinburgh in 1979 and currently resides there, working also as a furniture maker. She has a Joint Honors BA in Russian and Arabic (2004) and an MA in Applied Translation Studies (Arabic-English) (2006), both from the University of Leeds.

Rym Jalil is a writer and poet based in Cairo. They wrote their first poem at the age of nine. Rym's first published poem "Higher Power," a collaboration with Sara Fakhry Ismail, was a loose-leaf silk screen artist publication in an edition of 35. "Higher Power" was released as part of a series of events on independent publishing at Cairo Image Collective in September 2020. Most recently, they worked alongside other artists and writers eventually leading to a collective online publication "Bodies Breathing Under Water," which featured three of their poems. In their poetry, mostly written in Egyptian dialect, they use autobiographical events and abstract imagery interchangeably.

Qassim Majeed is an Iraqi poet from Baghdad. He authored numerous collections of poetry and was recognized in Iraq and in the Arab Gulf States for his talents. Qassim writes about contemporary Iraq and the effect of the post-war violence and conflict on the Iraqi public.

Maheera Migdadi is a writer and academic from Jordan currently living in Dammam, Saudi Arabia. She has a master's degree in finance and banking, and works as a lecturer at Imam Abdulrahman Bin Faisal University. Migdadi published her first short story collection, *And Then the Poppy Became Red*, in Jordan in 2010, and her second collection, *His Beautiful Things*, in Saudi Arabia in 2021. She has also published her work in various newspapers, magazines, and online platforms, including *Al Ra'i*, *Al-Quds*, *Alkalima*, and others.

Shakir Mustafa is a teaching professor of Arabic at Northeastern University who grew up in Iraq and taught at Mosul University for eleven years. He taught at Indiana University and Boston University from 1999 to 2008. His most recent book is *Contemporary Iraqi Fiction: An Anthology* (Syracuse, 2008; AUC 2009; paperback, 2018). Other book publications are in the areas of literary translation, Irish drama, and Jewish American fiction.

Nawal Nasrallah is an independent scholar, previously professor of English at the universities of Baghdad and Mosul. She has published books and articles on the history and culture of Middle-Eastern and Arab food, including *Delights from the Garden of Eden* (Authorhouse 3003, Equinox 2013), *Dates: A Global History* (Reaktion Books 2011), and English translations of medieval Arabic cookbooks, *Annals of the Caliphs' Kitchens* (Brill 2007), *Treasure Trove of Benefits and Varieties at the Table* (Brill 2017), and *Best of Delectable Foods and Dishes*, by Andalusi scholar Ibn Razin al-Tujibi (Brill 2021).

Michael Payne is a postdoctoral researcher at Ludwig-Maximilians-Universität München where he is a part of the European Research Council Project on Animals in Philosophy of the Islamic World. In 2020, he received his PhD from Brown University's Department of Religious Studies, and wrote a dissertation about al-Jahiz and human difference. He is a scholar of early Islam and late antique Christianity who specializes in the history of kalam, animals, and race. Currently, he's writing a book about al-Jahiz and working on a translation of his "Book of Mules."

Said Takieddine (1904–1960) was a Lebanese playwright, author, journalist, activist, and businessman.

Maisaa Tanjour is a freelance translator and researcher. She was born in Syria in 1979 and currently resides in Leeds. She is also an interpreter with years of experience working in diverse professional, humanitarian, local, and multicultural communities and organizations. She studied at the University of Homs, and has a BA in English Language and Literature and a PG Diploma in Literary Studies. She came to the UK in 2005 to study at the University of Leeds, and has an MA in Interpreting and Translation Studies, and a PhD in Translation Studies.

Katherine Van de Vate translates modern Arabic literature into English. She previously worked as an Arabic curator at the British Library and as a US diplomat, serving tours in Jordan, Egypt, the United Arab Emirates, Turkey, the UK, and Syria. Her translations have been published in *ArabLit Quarterly*, *Words without Borders*, and *Asymptote*.

Printed in Great Britain
by Amazon